CW00869685

286

Dear Pitman Publishing Customer

IMPORTANT – Read This Now!

We are delighted to announce a special free service for all of our customers.

Simply complete this form and return it to the address overleaf to receive:

A Free Customer Newsletter

B Free Information Service

C Exclusive Customer Offers – which have included free software, videos and relevant products

D Opportunity to take part in product development sessions

E The chance for you to write about your own business experience and become one of our respected authors

Fill this in now and return it to us (no stamp needed in the UK) to join our customer information service.

Name: _____ Position: _____

Company/Organisation: _____

Address (including postcode): _____

_____ Country: _____

Telephone: _____ Fax: _____

Nature of business: _____

Title of book purchased: _____

Comments: _____

_____

- | **Fold Here Then Staple** | -

We would be very grateful if you could answer these questions to help us with market research.

1 Where/How did you hear of this book?

☐ in a bookshop

☐ in a magazine/newspaper
(please state which):

_____

☐ information through the post

☐ recommendation from a colleague

☐ other (please state which):

_____

2 Which newspaper(s)/magazine(s) do you read regularly?:

_____

_____

3 When buying a business book which factors influence you most?
(Please rank in order)

☐ recommendation from a colleague

☐ price

☐ content

☐ recommendation in a bookshop

☐ author

☐ publisher

☐ title

☐ other(s):

_____

4 Is this book a

☐ personal purchase?

☐ company purchase?

5 Would you be prepared to spend a few minutes talking to our customer services staff to help with product development?
YES/NO

The Business Publisher

Written for managers competing in today's tough business world, our books will help you get the edge on competitors by showing you how to:

- increase quality, efficiency and productivity throughout your organisation
- use both proven and innovative management techniques
- improve the management skills of you and your staff
- implement winning customer strategies

In short they provide concise, practical information that you can use every day to improve the success of your business.

FINANCIAL TIMES

PITMAN PUBLISHING

the Institute
of Management
FOUNDATION

PITMAN
PUBLISHING

The Manager
as Coach

The Manager as Coach

Developing Your Team for Maximum Performance

JIM DURCAN
& DAVID OATES

FINANCIAL TIMES

PITMAN PUBLISHING

PITMAN PUBLISHING
128 Long Acre, London WC2E 9AN

A Division of Longman Group Limited

First published in Great Britain 1994

© Jim Durcan and David Oates 1994

British Library Cataloguing in Publication Data
A CIP catalogue record for this book can be obtained from the British Library.

ISBN 0 273 60464 3

Phototypeset in Linotron Times Roman by
Northern Phototypesetting Co. Ltd, Bolton
Printed and bound in Great Britain by
Biddles Ltd, Guildford and King's Lynn

10 9 8 7 6 5 4 3 2

CONTENTS

Preface   vii

1   THE PACE OF CHANGE   1

2   THE IMPACT OF EMPOWERMENT   15
    Case study Nuclear Electric   41
    Case study BP Exploration (BPEX)   55

3   THE CHANGING ROLE OF THE MANAGER   63

4   COACHING IN SPORT AND BUSINESS   93

5   COACHING TO SUIT THE SITUATION   113

6   CALAIS LOOP AND OTHER MESSAGES   139

7   COACHING TEAMS   157
    Case study Nuclear Electric   173
    Case study Royal Mail   181

8   PREPARING THE GROUND (TRAINING)   191
    Case study ICI Merseyside   197
    Case study Woolwich Building Society   210

**9   THE CHARACTERISTICS OF THE MANAGEMENT
     COACH**   219

Index   230

PREFACE

Coaching has been around for as long as men and women have competed on the sportsfield. Its introduction to the business arena is more recent. A combination of factors are persuading a growing number of organisations that the manager's role should change from that of hands-on controller to that of coach and facilitator.

Rapidly changing markets and technologies and the trend to globalisation all mean that organisations need to be more flexible and proactive. The old hierarchical structures that have served organisations well for 2,000 years are no longer appropriate for the business world of today. The old command and control structures are simply too slow to meet the needs of our swiftly changing times.

Delayering is greatly reducing middle management ranks and some trail-blazing organisations have turned their pyramidal structures upside down to ensure that the focus is on the front-line employees and the customers they serve. This is bringing about a complete reversal of the manager-subordinate relationship. Where subordinates used to be organised to serve the needs of management, the reverse is beginning to be the case.

For this fundamental shift of balance to succeed, front-line employees need to be empowered to take the initiatives demanded by their more critical role in the organisation. This places great strains on both the employees, who are accustomed to the rules of the old command and control organisations, and on managers, who are uncertain of what precisely is expected of them as coaches in this brave new world.

Inevitably there is resistance from both sides. Many managers, fearing loss of power and status, would prefer to cling on to their familiar roles, and employees are wondering what they are likely to gain from contributing in a more meaningful way to the companies that employ them. They often feel they are betraying their fellow workers by crossing over into areas previously regarded as the exclusive domain of management.

Nobody under-estimates the effort that is needed to make empowerment and coaching work. A growing number of pioneering organisations are proving, however, that there is much to be gained in taking this radically new path. Organisations as diverse as Barclays Bank, Woolwich Building Society, ICI, shoe firm Clarks International, Sainsbury's and Kent County Constabulary all claim substantial benefits from coaching.

Perhaps not surprisingly, some of these organisations have turned to former sports coaches to help them find the way forward. A number of sports stars have set up consultancies to pass on to business the lessons they have learned from being at the top of their fields of endeavour. For example, David Whitaker, who coached the English hockey team to a gold medal at the Seoul Olympics, has teamed up with Olympic hurdler David Hemery and former European saloon car champion Sir John Whitmore to form Performance Consultants.

The consultancy has devised a step-by-step coaching approach to help managers solve a range of problems. The authors of this book also offer a staged approach to coaching based on the CALAIS loop. While this is not a scientifically evaluated method, we hope that it will help to clarify the issues that are thrown up by management coaching. Like all evolving techniques, coaching has attracted a lot of controversy and opinions differ on how appropriate it is in different circumstances of business life.

Performance Consultants promote a system that encourages managers and employees to find their own solutions to problems. This is a long way from the 'telling' style of management that tends to characterise hierarchical organisations. But others caution that employees, used to their subordinate role in command and control organisations, cannot be expected overnight to take on their shoulders the management burdens that have tested experienced executives for decades.

Companies like Nuclear Electric, BP and Rank Xerox, who have shown the courage to bite the bullet, are demonstrating, however, that when managers coach their teams well, front-line staff can achieve goals previously undreamt of and which can be critical to the survival of those organisations.

Those managers who have been prepared to switch to the coaching approach are enjoying rewards they would not have thought possible. Not least of these is the pleasure of seeing their teams perform a more fulfilling function in the operations which dominate their working lives. This book is an attempt to chronicle some of these pioneering success stories in the hope that they will pave the way for those organisations yet to start out on this hazardous but exciting journey of discovery.

1

THE PACE OF CHANGE

The late 1980s and the 1990s have witnessed extraordinary organisational changes. These changes have affected the size and competitiveness of markets, the rate of technological progress, the reduction in the role of the state in economic life and the nature of organisations themselves.

Organisations have been transformed in a tidal wave of downsizing and delayering, mergers and de-mergers, joint ventures and partnerships which has fundamentally altered the nature of business life. The old 'command and control' structures with their rigid hierarchies, their chains of command, their boss-subordinate fiefdoms and their implicit assumptions that the purpose of management was 'to tell other people what to do and make sure they did it' are being challenged by new and more flexible forms of organisation.

These new flexible forms fundamentally alter the nature of managerial tasks. These new organisations understand that their competitiveness depends on their ability to learn; that learning must be grounded in the present and the future, not the past; and that learning must be undertaken by all the members of the organisation and not just a small group of senior executives at the centre. Learning is not the acquiring of a lifetime's experience; learning is responding positively and constructively to current and potential events. Learning is not an individual indulgence; but a necessary team responsibility.

Confronted by these changes, many managers find that they need to alter fundamentally their approach to their role. Their primary task has become that of developing the capability and performance of their teams to achieve standards and levels previously undreamt of. Such developmental activity – increasingly known as coaching – poses new demands on managers and their teams. Managers who were appointed because of their expertise or their ability 'to make things happen' are discovering that their expertise is obsolete and that it is not they but their teams 'who make things happen'.

A number of factors have combined to bring about this fundamental change of approach in the way companies are being managed.

NEW TECHNOLOGY

There are significant changes in the business environment that are combining to make life far more complex for organisations. Change is happening far more rapidly, particularly in relation to new technology. New product development, and the updating of existing products to compete more vigorously in the market place, are taking place at a much faster rate. Patterns of technological change, such as the microchip revolution, mean that complete processes are being abandoned. The development of new materials has transformed production possibilities.

This was an issue highlighted at the Offshore Europe conference organised by the Society of Petroleum Engineers in Aberdeen in September 1993. A paper prepared by oil technicians and supervisors working on a BP production platform noted:

> Today's businesses often have to operate in an environment of constant and sometimes dramatic change. Change driven by the chaos of competition, of technological advance, the vagaries of the domestic economy and increasingly, the global market place. More and more organisations are focusing their efforts in emphasising continuous process improvement, in the service of increased return to customers, shareholders and employees. The prime prerequisite for these objectives is valuing, developing and fully utilising the skills and the competencies of the whole work force.

GLOBAL COMPETITION

To compound the problems brought about by technological change, organisations are having to face up to the existence of global competition on a scale that has never been known before, which is mainly a function of bigger firms. Differential rates of growth between regions of the world have forced firms to expand to avoid being left behind. Lower communication costs and dramatic improvements in communication quality have reduced the difficulties of operating globally. The growth of the mass media has swung the balance of difficulty in favour of opening up new markets. Lower trade barriers and rising national incomes have raised the attractiveness of operating globally. This is likely to be accelerated by the Group of Seven discussions which took place in Tokyo in July 1993, and made significant strides in reducing trade barriers between the leading industrialised countries of the world in the hope of stimulating economic growth.

SHIFTS IN CONSUMER EXPECTATIONS

It is also possible to detect a major shift in customer or consumer expectations. Recent experience of change – including the rapid obsolescence of new purchases – allied to constant reports of product innovations, developments and advances have dramatically raised expectations of what products and services ought to be available. The increase in these expectations may be so rapid as to be exponential. Therefore, the pressure on firms to adapt to those demands is increasing all the time or they risk losing sales because customers prefer to wait for a more advanced product announced but not yet produced by a competitor.

When the changes in technology, consumer tastes and in global competition are linked together, firms find themselves inhabiting a world in which change is happening at a pace never experienced before. Things that previously only changed every ten years are now changing in the space of two years. A year may still contain 365 or 366 days but it is much shorter than it used to be. This sheer pace of change is quite frightening.

CHAOS

The other factor that organisations are having to grapple with is that the world has become more turbulent and less predictable. Business has never operated in accordance with a highly defined pattern of cause and effect. Even the best planned change had unforeseen side effects as well as occasional unforeseen major consequences. If you add change to change the results are inevitably unpredictable. Companies find themselves in a situation that resembles chaos. It is much more difficult to predict the outcomes of events which impact on a firm's operations. At the same time, it is virtually impossible to predict the impact of the firm's own actions.

That has some significant implications for firms operating in the global arena. In the past they might have considered making major investment decisions assuming that these could be recouped within a fifteen year time span. Today, the size of such investments is magnified by the demands of the global market, while the predictability of the returns is transmuted by the chaos factor. Playing roulette blindfold with chips of indeterminate value would seem safe in comparision.

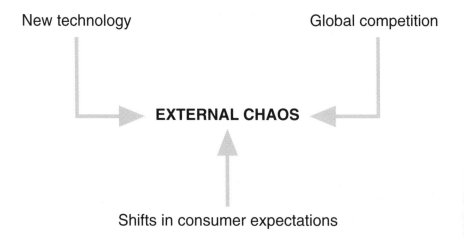

Fig. 1.1   External chaos

Seeking projects with a shorter payback period, in a world with globally efficient capital markets, simply increases the required rate of profitability which in turn may reflect the perceived riskiness of the project. Smaller investments – whether in capital projects or training – reduce the strategic risks. They may also reduce the global reach of such investments and the revenue streams generated.

All these pressures mean that firms have to be much more flexible in terms of their ability to adapt to change, much more responsive to what is actually happening out there in the market place and much more creative, because they will be required to a much greater extent to cope with problems that they have never encountered before. They cannot rely on experience. They must depend on creativity to overcome the unpredictable changes that will inevitably assail them.

COMMAND AND CONTROL

All of that is a fairly heady mixture. If organisations try to meet all those pressures with the old command and control approach to management they will soon be in trouble. The conventional hierarchical approach is heavily segmented by function. Each function has a particular set of activities. They perform their set of duties and when completed they are passed on to the next group. Responsibility is transferred with the task.

The linkages are vertical. You go up and down in your function; you don't go across. Formal cross-functional linkages only occur at senior levels of the organisation. That means instructions and messages from the top of the hierarchy take a long time to reach the bottom and vice-versa; sometimes they never get there at all. This is hardly fitting to a world that demands high flexibility and high levels of responsiveness.

The creativity in this style of management depends on the capacity of the people at the top of the pyramid. The people at the top reached there because they were highly experienced. What was valued about them was their experience, but their experience – especially if it relates to just one function – may be much less relevant in a rapidly changing world. The people who are more likely to be able to be creative are those closer to the task, who can actually see what is happening in the market and are better placed to understand what the customers actually want.

All these factors taken together amount to a powerful case for decentralisation, ensuring that the power is shifted out from the centre and downwards. Power must shift not just from a centralised profit or cost centre to a localised one, but to the front-line troops. Simply doing that does not spark the kind of creativity or responsiveness that companies need in today's world. Firms may achieve more flexibility by breaking the previous operating unit into twelve sub-units. Each of the sub-units is likely to be capable of responding more flexibly in its own environment, but that in itself does not create greater responsiveness. The messages may still be ignored. Nor does it necessarily produce creative responses. If management in the sub-units see decentralisation as an opportunity to command and control their own small hierarchy there is little gain in organisational adaptability.

CREATIVE SOLUTIONS

Increasingly, companies are turning to empowerment, which aims to devolve authority for taking personal initiatives to the front-line troops, as the way to generate the kind of awareness of issues and their creative solution necessary for companies' survival into the next century. BP, for example, is involving its operators in the quest for creative ideas to extend the life span of its major oil fields in the North Sea and Alaska. Nuclear Electric, which faces the prospect of having to turn multi-million pound losses into profits without government subsidy, has similarly co-opted the creative power of its work force by forming empowered teams in the quest for greater efficiency and productivity.

Previous experience does not tell either of these organisations how to solve the major challenges they need to address. There is no blueprint to tell them the way forward. It is only by tapping the collective imaginations of their front-line staff that they are likely to come up with the kind of quantum-leap solutions that will ensure their survival. As one BP executive puts it, 'With every pair of hands comes a brain.'

These organisations are attempting to tap the intellectual capacity that is otherwise ignored. They realise that you will only get the high-speed responsiveness required today by giving responsibility to those closest to the problem.

BETTER EDUCATED WORK FORCE

The UK, like many other European countries, is seeing an ever higher proportion of graduates entering the workforce. A more educated workforce almost certainly means that there are more employees who are unprepared simply to do what they are told and who want the freedom and the responsibility to respond to situations, to take initiatives and achieve results. These pressures may have been tempered somewhat by the impact of the recession on new graduates, which leaves many desperate to work, but such short-term effects should not obscure the long-term trends.

LESS JOB SECURITY

In the past employees often endured autocratic organisations because they enjoyed job security. That is no longer true. The recession and the drive to make organisations leaner and more competitive has put paid to job security and without it employees naturally look for other compensations. They are less likely to be tolerant of organisations that tie them down to rigid procedures and discourage individual initiatives. Employment will be seen less as a career and more as an opportunity to further develop marketable skills. Note the BP oil workers in the paper presented to the Offshore Europe conference:

> It has now become clear that in future companies are unlikely to be able to offer lifetime security of employment. This is reflected in the commitment employees are prepared to give. For the company, the return on human investment is a direct function of the value placed upon them. For

employees, autonomy, increased responsibility, involvement in the decision process, challenge, skills growth and personal marketability, as well as financial reward, are the new values.

LESS AWE OF AUTHORITY

In general, there is less awe of authority today than in past generations. Parental control has gradually been eroded since Victorian times and there is evidence of much less respect for authority in schools and other institutions. There are growing signs that royalty is not looked up to in the way that it was.

In the world at large, we have witnessed in recent years the fall of one despotic regime after another in the former Eastern Europe. People-power has taken over from tyranny. While in the more affluent nations of the West, the urge to rebel and be assertive may not be quite so strong, there is no doubt that the acceptance of authority is no longer automatic. People want a greater say in their own destinies and want the freedom to act according to their own judgements.

This trend has some unfortunate repercussions. Police forces all over Britain are struggling to maintain the rule of law, which is an essential ingredient of democracy. There is what could be interpreted as a sinister trend towards members of the public taking matters into their own hands and forming vigilante forces to police their own communities. But anarchy has its positive aspects as well. When people feel they have (the freedom to express themselves, they make a far more valuable contribution to society than if they are merely cogs in an established machine.

It is perhaps no coincidence that people power is a growing phenomenon at a time when US management guru Warren Bennis is alerting the world to the consequences of an apparently universal leadership vacuum. President Clinton and Prime Minister John Major have shared the dubious distinction of being the lowest rated leaders since polls began.

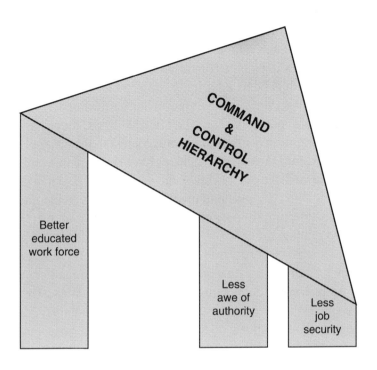

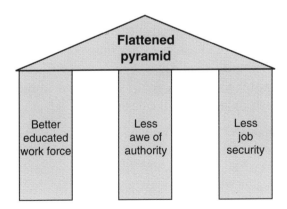

Fig. 1.2   The flattening of the pyramid

THE FLATTENING OF THE PYRAMID

For years management gurus have been predicting the demise of autocratic management and the pyramidal organisation structure. The pyramid has taken a long time to crumble. The ancient Chinese invented it as a way to pass instructions down the line and information up to the top. It has been adopted by the military, the Church and latterly by public services and commercial organisations.

In recent years, particularly in the United States, there have been numerous experiments with new organisational shapes to replace the ubiquitous pyramid. The new structures have rejoiced in wonderfully evocative names like *the beehive, the bell, the doughnut* and *the bicycle wheel*. They have all had much the same aim of moving away from the sharp-pointed pyramid with its traditional hierarchical approach to management.

Shortly after BP introduced its Project 1990 initiative to create a new company culture, it attempted to redraw its organisation chart in terms of empowered teams built around company assets. The result was what one BP executive describes as a mass of 'brightly coloured Easter eggs'. The purpose of the exercise was not to pigeon-hole everyone in the organisation, as in the old hierarchical structure, but to emphasise to managers throughout the group that BP had arrived at a new era in terms of the way it was going to be run. It was the visualisation of a new style of management that stressed the need to place the authority into the hands of the people handling the company's enormous range of assets rather than concentrating power at the top of the pyramid.

The radical switch to flatter organisations is probably best summed up by Tom Peters, co-author of the bestseller *In Search of Excellence*:

Whole new shapes of organisations are starting to emerge. Look at the new upstarts in Great Britain, to some extent, and in the US, to a great extent, and they just don't look like yesterday's companies in any way, shape or form. The way people look, smell and spend their day is not the way they have done so for perhaps the last couple of thousand years.

EMPOWERMENT

Empowerment is rapidly becoming the buzz-word of the 1990s. But more importantly, it is re-shaping organisations and radically changing the boss-subordinate relationship in companies and many other organisations. The familiar command and control operating mode, typical of the pyramidal organisation structure, is giving way to a counselling and coaching style of management.

To facilitate this fundamental shift, some organisations are turning their pyramidal organisation structures upside down so that the focus is on those employees who interface directly with customers and suppliers. Self-managed work groups – some of them leaderless – are also being introduced.

This stark departure from entrenched traditional management practices is throwing up a lot of controversial issues. Are front-line staff capable of taking advantage of the newfound authority that is being devolved to them? Do they want to take initiatives outside the scope of their job description? How much personal initiative can they take without overstepping the line? Can they be expected to understand the full implications of the corporate mission?

Even more crucial, will managers be able to adapt to the new coaching and counselling style that is required of them? Indeed, will there be any jobs left for them to do if self-managed work groups become the norm?

WHAT IS EMPOWERMENT?

Empowerment basically means embuing staff with sufficient self-confidence and skill/competence that they are able to exercise discretion – individually or jointly – and resolve issues which would otherwise have been referred elsewhere (upwards or sideways in the organisation) for a decision, or even just ignored. This process 'enables' staff by removing constraints – organisational and personal – from them and giving them greater control over their own destinies. Seen in this way, empowerment as a process aims to alleviate or remove employees' feelings that they are powerless and that their work has little or no meaning. Empowerment is, consequently, far more than delegation; it is about emancipating staff and revolutionising their attitudes towards work.

WHY ENGAGE IN EMPOWERMENT?

Six major reasons are apparent:

- the increasing pace of change, the turbulence of the environment, the speed of competitive responses, the acceleration of customer demands and the ever-growing thicket of regulation and legislation require a speed and flexibility of response which is incompatible with the old style command and control model of organisational function
- organisations themselves are changing; the impact of downsizing, delayering and decentralising means that the old methods of achieving co-ordination and control are no longer appropriate. To achieve performance in these new circumstances requires that staff take and exercise much more responsibility
- organisations require much more cross-functional working, much more co-operation between areas, much more integration in their processes if they are to meet their customer needs. Such co-operation can be achieved through empowerment
- staff are no longer prepared to accept the old command and control systems. Much wider availability of education, greater emphasis on lifetime development and the end of the old certainties of job security and steady advancement have contributed to a situation where jobs are valued for the development opportunities that they offer rather than in themsleves. Organisations which fail to meet these aspirations will not receive the performance they require and will suffer a continuous haemorrhaging of their staff
- really good managerial talent is increasingly perceived as scarce and expensive. Using it for direct supervision of staff able to manage themselves compounds these difficulties. Really good managerial talent can be focused more on the external challenges and less on internal problem solving, more on the long-term issues and less on firefighting

- empowerment may uncover sources of managerial talent which were previously unrecognised because it creates circumstances in which that talent can be revealed and given the opportunity to flourish.

FORMS OF EMPOWERMENT

The debate here reflects the kinds of issues which used to be talked about in relation to employee participation. Empowerment may focus on the job or the wider organisation. Job-focused empowerment increases staff autonomy and discretion and range of task in carrying out their responsibilities but retains significant elements of the old command and control systems by defining those responsibilities. In effect this form of empowerment revisits some of the job design issues and favours greater autonomy, discretion and variety. It also acknowledges the inevitable limits of individuals' capabilities and fosters teamworking to increase the capability available.

Such empowerment does not necessarily resolve some of the wider organisational issues. In tackling issues beyond the immediate job, the scope for empowerment appears to stretch from suggestion schemes to self-managing work teams which are responsible for a whole area of business or customers, from supplier to final delivery. These latter forms of empowerment may require extensive re-skilling before they can take off.

APPROPRIATE CIRCUMSTANCES FOR EMPOWERMENT?

Empowerment is more than just another form of organisation. It is the expression of a set of values which regards people as assets rather than costs, which values their contributions, trusts their judgements and acknowledges openly that seniority is no guarantee of judgement. It may be possible, given an appropriate set of values, to empower all staff in all organisations. In the interim, before that revolution in values occurs, some ground is likely to prove more fertile and some more stony. Among the more fertile the following conditions are likely to be met:

- nature of business and business strategy, e.g. differentiation through personal service and customisation
- extended, intensive involvement with customers
- complex, non-routine technology requiring high level skills and continual adjustment and involvement
- instability and unpredictability of the business environment
- extent to which organisational culture and managerial style are disposed towards empowerment
- extent to which the existing workforce wants or is suited to empowerment.

In the next two chapters we look at how empowerment is impacting on the way that organisations are run and how it is changing the role of the manager.

2

THE IMPACT OF EMPOWERMENT

When Alistair Wright was appointed human resource director of Digital Equipment Co., UK subsidiary of the world's third largest computer manufacturer, he vowed he would set an example for the rest of the organisation by passing authority down the line and totally empowering his staff. But it was easier said than done. Wright discovered that you can't hand out authority like luncheon vouchers. The motivation for taking personal initiatives has to come from the employees themselves.

Recalls Wright, 'I used to think you could just sprinkle golden dust on their heads and say 'you are now empowered – go away and multiply'. It doesn't work, because they are so constrained by the existing paradigm. It took me a long time to learn a fundamental truth about empowerment. You can't give it; people have to take it.'

Wright's experience underscores a concern that many organisations have about empowerment. If you empower front-line employees to take personal initiatives beyond the boundaries of their routine tasks, firstly you need to know that they are willing and able to do so. Secondly, how do they know how far they can go?

Empowerment enthusiasts say it is all to do with company culture and ensuring that employees are fully conversant with the corporate goals and mission. But is that realistic? Can a cleaner on the shopfloor be expected to become fully versed in the complex set of aims a major corporation is driven by? Certainly a growing number of organisations are trying hard to achieve just that.

A British management researcher visiting the United States recently listened enthralled as the chauffeur driving him to Kennedy

Airport ran through the detailed mission statement of the leading American hospital that employed him. The British visitor had just heard the exact same overview from the hospital's top administrator. The chauffeur told the Englishman that everyone at the hospital was regularly updated on any changes to the hospital's corporate goals.

COMPETING WITH THE EAST

Like a lot of innovative management thinking, empowerment has its roots in the United States. It has been used for more than a century in political circles in the US to describe the gaining of power, especially by minority groups, but has taken on new significance recently as a result of the desire among American corporations to find a way to compete more effectively with their rivals from the Far East. Those charged with running American industry took a long hard look at the way Japanese firms operate and tried to understand what it was that made them so much more productive and successful. The overriding conclusion was that the Japanese make a much better job of winning the commitment of their employees at all levels.

The problem for the West, however, is that Japanese culture reflects not just different behaviours but different values and different assumptions about the world. American culture, for example, is epitomised by the archctypal hero – the lone cowboy who goes off to fight the Red Indians. Its values are those of individualism, individual initiative, individual effort and individual reward. In Japanese culture, on the other hand, the individual is subordinated to the collective effort. Teamwork and unselfish dedication are the way to achieve collectively set goals. This is far more than a matter of a particular management technique. It reflects differences of history, tradition, location, experience and values.

That does not mean, however, that lessons cannot be learned from the Japanese success story. It is impractical to replicate Eastern culture in the West, but there may be much to be gained from extracting certain elements of that culture and adapting them to the Western way of life. In their search for the key ingredients of the Japanese model, the Americans concluded that empowerment is an important aspect of achieving greater productivity from their work force.

TAYLORIAN MODELS

When, for example, they compared the efficiency of US factories with those in Japan, they discovered that the American plants were still heavily influenced by Taylorian models of work organisation. In those areas where unionism is still an influence Taylorism was reflected in tightly circumscribed jobs and fixed procedures. There was nothing in the way of flexible working, multi-skilling and employee responsiveness. When cost patterns at US auto factories were compared with those of their Japanese counterparts, there appeared little hope that the American car industry could survive the severe competition.

Not everyone is convinced that empowerment holds the key for putting the West on a more competitive footing with the East. There are those like Bernard Taylor, professor of business policy at Henley Management College, who raise serious doubts:

> When I hear the word empowerment, I reach for my gun, because it's one of those cosy words. It's like new bottles for old wine. I like the idea of delegation because it's a clean word. Empowerment is rather a dirty word.

Clean or dirty, there is more general agreement that organisations can *disempower* people. It is a simple matter to create an organisational culture that says never take chances, always cover your back, always put everything in writing and always make sure you have authority. All that can disempower people. It may disempower the whole organisation; everyone may feel that they are unable to exercise power. Empowerment calls for the creation of organisational structures that make it easier to delegate, but the initiative largely has to come from those whose talents the organisation is trying to release. That need for upward reach and grasp differentiates empowerment sharply from delegation. Managers may delegate to their staff. Staff may empower themselves – but only in an appropriate institutional setting.

INVERTING THE PYRAMID

Such reservations are doing nothing to dent the enthusiasm of the growing band of organisations that are embracing empowerment wholeheartedly. Companies like Rank Xerox are so dedicated to the idea that they are inverting their organisation structures to ensure that the front-line troops – those who interface most closely with the customer – become the focus of attention. Senior managers at Rank Xerox and other companies, like BP and Sherwood Computer Services, are being turned into coaches. Their job is no longer to control and command; it is to provide support to the newly-empowered front-line employees. Costly training programmes have been introduced to help top executives make this, often traumatic, transformation.

Rank Xerox is one of the companies that openly admits it has embraced empowerment in order to compete with the Japanese. Observes Vernon Zelmer, the Canadian managing director of Rank Xerox (UK) Ltd.:

> We learned very quickly when we benchmarked the Japanese that the companies that were starting to whip our hides were those moving away from the pyramidal hierarchy. They were moving towards a process-driven, customer-focused organisation. So we tipped the pyramid upside down. The customer is at the top. We have a hundred thousand hearts and minds around the world focused on the customer.

Professor Rosabeth Moss Kanter, of Harvard Business School, argues that empowerment can only work when radical changes are made to traditional hierarchical structures. She described three such new structures in a speech she made to a national conference of the Institute of Personnel Management in 1992. These were highlighted in an article by Godfrey Golzen in the 15 November 1992, issue of *The Sunday Times*:

- **Upside-Down**. Instead of headquarters staff telling production units and people at the customer interface what to do, they act as their support. In some companies, according to Kanter, organisation charts are being re-drawn with the chief executive at the bottom.

- **Inside-out**. The traditional basis for organisations was that customers were kept at arm's length, but the employer-employee bond was sacrosanct. Now almost the reverse is true; customers are brought in as partners and allies. They are even trained by suppliers to make sure they have the right skills.
- **Horizontal** rather than vertical. Old-style organisations are marked by what Kanter calls 'the elevator-and-wall mentality'. You worked your way upwards to the executive suite and crossed physical barriers to get to other departments. Now organisations consist of teams, project groups and task forces rather than departmental empires. 'People used to work to get a title; now they work to achieve a result,' she suggests.

Such ideas may seem simple in concept but resistance to their practical implementation remains strong. The hierarchical organisation has been around for so long it is seen as part of the natural order. Suggesting hierarchies are inappropriate has the same power to shock as suggesting that the sun did not go round the earth in sixteenth century Europe. Not only do such ideas threaten conceptual confusion, they imperil the very power structures through which decision makers operate. Some organisations have made or are making the required shifts in conceptual and organisational structures.

SELF-MANAGED WORK GROUPS

A number of trail-blazing organisations are setting up self-managed work groups, some of them leaderless. Senior managers, now acting as coaches, only intervene when the work teams run into difficulties with which they seem unable to cope. The coaches move in temporarily, like a pilot going on board a ship to guide it through particularly difficult waters.

London-based Sherwood Computer Services has replaced its former hierarchical structure with fourteen self-managed client teams that report directly to the board. They have been empowered to make their own decisions and run their operations the way they see fit within an overall corporate plan. Says Bob Thomas, the computer firm's ex-chairman, 'There was an enormous need to improve our service to our clients, and balanced teams – balanced in skill terms, having everything within them to serve the needs of a small group of clients – seemed the way to bring that about.'

The teams were formed around the clients that Sherwood had in January 1991 when the new corporate structure was introduced. The company's three main customer groups are Lloyds of London, insurance companies and local authorities. Sherwood has hardly any central services. The accountants and book-keepers who used to provide a central service have been distributed among the client teams. Only a finance director and one assistant remain at the centre.

From time to time the accountants detach themselves from their various client teams and form what Sherwood calls a *virtual team* to tackle a particular project affecting the company as a whole.

Since there were not enough accountants to go round, some teams have had to do without. In the teams that were not allocated a central office accountant, the skills have had to be developed among team members who were not previously experienced in that area. Explains Thomas, 'That was a deliberate act. Our policy was to upskill people in order to get through more work with the same number of staff.'

Rank Xerox has converted its entire customer service division into 250 self-managed work groups. Shaun Pantling, director of customer service, believes 'the opportunity for empowerment is practically limitless. We are now looking at the idea of team appraisals rather than appraising individuals. We are also looking at ways the team could actually carve up its own salary increases. Already most of the teams are responsible for things like reward and recognition.'

Digital Equipment's UK organisation in Reading has introduced self-management to around forty teams, covering such areas as finance, personnel, engineering and customer accounts. Elaborates Chris Lever, a human resource manager at Reading, 'We have given our account teams as much authority as we possibly can. We now call our account managers entrepreneurs because they are responsible for their own budgets and for how they spend and allocate their funds.'

Digital Equipment UK has set aside £1 million a year to hand out as cash rewards for outstanding performance. In the true spirit of empowerment, the company asks its employees to nominate those who they think most deserve to be recipients.

CAUTION

Some companies are embracing the new empowerment credo with more caution. At W.H. Smith, where attempts are being made to disperse authority to the outer reaches of the organisation's retail empire, the company is hedging its bets by devising a guide to decision making, which gives managers and employees some indication of the boundaries to their newfound freedom of action.

CIVIL SERVICE

Empowerment has even infiltrated the bureaucratic cages of the Civil Service, where a management revolution is currently underway. The government has decided that the Civil Service, which is responsible for such diverse activities as social security benefits, vehicle testing and printing passports, is too complex for central control. According to Sir Peter Butler, head of the Civil Service, the main thrust of the management revolution is 'to delegate powers to take decisions as close as possible to the point of delivery.'

The Benefits Agency is typical of the kind of management shake-up being introduced. In the past, benefits offices have tended to be battle-grounds between staff and claimants. Now the aim is to treat claimants as customers whose wishes are paramount within the over-all guidelines of government policy and departmental regulation. The agency is measuring performance against customer service targets and staff are being given greater freedom to take initiatives. Notes Michael Bichard, chief executive of the Benefits Agency:

> People at every level, from supervisor to senior manager, wanted more responsibility, more freedom to take decisions and not actually be governed by what was a very bureaucratic top-heavy management. Although some people found these changes uncomfortable, particularly those used to being told how to do things, the vast majority more than appreciates the changes that have happened.

OPPORTUNITIES TO STRETCH

There is ample evidence to suggest that in an organisation that empowers them to do so, many employees would welcome the opportunity to expand the narrow scope of their routine work. There is also every indication that employees in mundane jobs are capable of being stretched. Management guru Tom Peters cites the example of an American sausage factory to make this point. Ten workers performing the most menial tasks imaginable were picked from the processing line. All but two of them were found to be leading personal lives that were full of achievement. Two of them had built their own homes. Another was a leading light opera singer in her local community. Another ran a youth club. Most of the activities that characterised their social life involved management skills and the ability to run budgets, which in the business context has always been regarded as the exclusive province of senior executives. Peters asks the highly relevant question: 'why do so many workers leave their talents at the factory gate?'

Part of the problem, as Wright of Digital Equipment discovered, is that employees have grown used over many years to the idea that they are not supposed to take initiatives. They have learned to play their part in the hierarchy. Their role has been to receive instructions and carry them out according to strict rules and regulations.

HIDDEN TALENTS

Research by Sainsbury's, the leading retail group, among its staff, reveals that although many people have hidden talents they often lack confidence in their ability to apply those talents in the work place. Observes Judith Evans, Sainsbury's director of corporate personnel:

> They don't necessarily see the relevance of them in the work place. We need to persuade people that they have talents which are of value to the organisation. So we've devised a staged process to tell people what's involved by using existing staff who have talents they use outside work, which they have decided to use inside work – people who perhaps

organise a local Beaver group (junior scouts). They have organisational skills and that's one of the skills we're interested in for the organisation.

Sainsbury's has devised a 'fun-type' questionnaire aimed at uncovering whether or not employees have attributes they use in their private lives which might possibly be used in the work context to the benefit of both the individual and the organisation. The ultimate intention is to identify employees with junior management potential or with specialist skills.

Empowerment is a cornerstone of Sainsbury's entire training and development approach. Says Evans, 'We realise that we're facing increased pace of change and we need to be increasingly competitive, that there is a wealth of talent in the organisation we are not tapping. We need to address their needs if we are going to ask them to contribute more.'

Evans admits that it is virtually impossible to measure the impact of the programmes Sainsbury's has put in place to achieve a more empowered work force. 'You can bandy figures around, but I don't think we could be confident about them enough to say we think it has led to a thirty per cent improvement in productivity. We haven't got the evidence to back it up. We know that in trials we have got benefits that are going to be worth significant amounts in terms of productivity.'

Evans is equally frank about the possible impact of empowerment on employee turnover. 'Our employee turnover has reduced quite significantly. Again, it's difficult to unravel the effects of the recession from our own actions. We hope it is as much our action as it is the recession. I know other organisations say that the reduction in their employee turnover is a result of personnel policies. I think we would be rather more cautious than that. But I do believe it is going to be important for moving out of the recession that we've worked on this area. It is perhaps at that stage that we can see whether it's made a difference.'

Retaining staff through empowerment runs counter to much received wisdom and expectation. Charles Handy has articulated a vision where almost all staff are self-employed seeking out those organisations which offer the greatest opportunity for self-development to improve future marketability. Others, including Nuclear Electric, have seen empowerment as a means of reducing headcount which, in the short term at least, means raising labour turnover. The reconciliation of these conflicts is that organisations in the future will need to attract the very best of the available talent to be highly competitive, and a key characteristic of the best available talent is those individuals' desire to learn and develop. The nature of the employment relationship is less important than the development and identification of talent.

EMPLOYABILITY

ICI's Chemicals and Polymers division at Merseyside has introduced a career development programme for shopfloor workers (see Chapter Seven) that helps them advance in the organisation. It invites shopfloor workers to map out their skills and try to match them with future ambitions. For John Williams, a process operator, the exercise was a real eye-opener:

> It really brings home to you that you've got so much more than you're giving to ICI. That was the kick-off point for me. It made me question why I was doing things outside work that they wouldn't let me do inside work. Why should I be content with doing things they think I can do instead of what I know I can do?

The ICI career development programme is aimed at broadening shopfloor workers' skills so that they can make a greater contribution towards the company's efficiency and competitiveness. But the company also runs a sponsorship scheme that allows a small number of employees to explore interests that are not necessarily directly related to their job. Austin Dunne, who works in the plant workshops at ICI Merseyside, was given the opportunity to spend two days a week for a year pursuing his interest in decorative ceramics. He buys and sells antique ceramics as a hobby and he wanted to learn more about the restoration side of the business. He believes the experience brought benefits for ICI as well as for himself:

> It not only builds up your skills; you get to meet people and it gives you

confidence; you get to know how things function outside ICI. That's also been beneficial at work, because I now have more confidence with people at work – with management. In the past I didn't have a lot of contact with management. If the manager wanted to see you, it was automatically assumed you'd done something wrong.

An increasing number of companies are providing facilities to help their employees broaden their skills in areas that are not necessarily related to their current job. These companies realise that while in a fast-changing world they can no longer guarantee a life-long company career, they can help to furnish employees with the broader skills that enhance their general chances of employment. Employability is a more important priority than tenure of service. In a fast-changing world it is more difficult for firms to predict the pool of skills that they will require. Enabling employees to develop new unrelated skills may be far more than raising individual employability.

FRESH START

It is far easier for a manager taking up a new post to empower his staff than someone who has to break away from established practices that have been the norm in the work place for many years. When Tony Grant was appointed to head the Royal Mail's main delivery office at Dorchester in 1992, he took the opportunity to empower the postal staff working there. Rather than assuming all the responsibilities of his predecessor in the job, Grant made an assessment of the capabilities of his staff and shared out many of the tasks that would previously have been regarded as his province. Says Grant, 'The basic idea was to come in and release control if you like – so release energy and just give people freedom to make decisions and to do things.'

Grant has found by trial and error that suddenly empowering employees can lead to complications. One front-line postman was released from normal duties for a few weeks to explore ways to improve one of the sorting processes. He was so enamoured by the prospect of taking on such a high-level responsibility that he 'took ownership' of the project and failed to seek the views of his colleagues to any real extent, causing some resentment among them and leaving them feeling anything but empowered.

But Grant has not regretted taking the empowerment route. For the most part, it has led to a much more efficient operation and a more fulfilled work force. He adds:

> Delegation can be interpreted as passing off work, but I basically shared out among the others all the day-to-day adminstrative tasks my predecessor undertook. I thought that the easiest way for me to achieve empowerment was not to learn those tasks in the first place. For example, the daily accounts are quite a major task in their own right. I delegated that to someone else in the organisation who was perfectly capable of doing it, because I didn't see that it should be my preserve.

Grant points out that the reorganisation of The Post Office has left many managers with little choice but to delegate to empowered staff. 'We've cut away several tiers of management, so that managers, even if they want to be autocratic, are going to find it difficult because they've got too many people to look after. They have to be supportive. We've put the structure in place to help that culture along.'

PRODUCTIVITY GAINS

Empowerment enthusiasts are being spurred on by stories of remarkable productivity gains. Research by Professor Quinn Mills, a US management expert at Harvard Business School, shows that organisations that unleash the creativity of their work force can routinely achieve productivity gains of between thirty and fifty per cent a year.

Examples abound of empowerment's potency for productive change. British Airways' engineering division, for example, set some cost saving targets to reduce overheads. Normally this would have been achieved by mandatory budget cuts. But seeking suggestions from front-line staff – maintenance and overhaul engineers – the company came up with savings that were three times greater than those targeted for.

Rank Xerox has recorded some significant productivity gains

among its self-managed service groups in the Netherlands. The service engineers operate in groups of between five and seven and control and determine their own tasks. They rotate the group leaders or co-ordinators about every six months. 'They actually own the customer base; they own the work processes and a lot of the measurement is done by themselves,' explains Ralph Orrico, executive director of group resources at the company's European headquarters in Marlow, Bucks.

The gains, according to Orrico, are manifold:

- Productivity has increased by ten per cent in two consecutive years. At Rank Xerox, productivity is measured in terms of how many photocopying machines, for example, are serviced per man over a given period of time.
- Unexpectedly, product performance has improved by eight per cent. That relates to the amount of time the machine is in working order, which is not an area that service engineers can always influence.
- Response times – how long it takes for an engineer to arrive on the job following a call to the service centre – has improved by thirty-four per cent. That has been influenced by the engineers working together to ensure that there is maximum coverage of the helpline.
- Broken calls have decreased by forty per cent. A broken call is when an engineer arrives to repair a machine and discovers that he has the wrong part or the wrong equipment to diagnose the fault and has to return to the service centre again before carrying out the repairs. Orrico describes the reduction as 'astounding', adding, 'clearly it's an expensive call when an engineer arrives and fails to fix something. It's also probably a big irritant to the customer.'
- The satisfaction of customers serviced by the Dutch engineers is at around ninety-eight per cent. Orrico suggests that the number of unsatisfied customers is probably less than two per cent, 'because you have a neutral zone in there as well'. The Dutch success augurs well for Rank Xerox's corporate goal to achieve a hundred per cent customer satisfaction by 1995.

CRISIS

Often it is when faced with an impending crisis or a momentous challenge that organisations turn to empowerment for their salvation. Paradoxically it can be fear that drives an empowerment programme – fear of the consequences if the organisation in question fails to adopt an innovative approach to an apparently intractable problem.

BP's exploration division has used empowered work teams to come up with ways to extend the life of declining oil fields in Alaska and the North Sea. The prospect of wholesale job losses is a powerful motivator and the people who are most likely to suffer the consequences – the oil workers themselves – are the most likely to come up with the kind of imaginative solutions that can turn impending disaster into a triumph of innovation.

Similarly, empowered teams at Nuclear Electric's Hartlepool station have been involved in finding ways to turn heavy financial losses into profits as a way to avoid the same fate as the local coal industry. In both cases, senior management set what appeared on the face of it to be impossible targets and left empowered teams to find the best route forward. (See case studies at the end of this chapter.)

GREENFIELD EMPOWERMENT

A greenfield site would seem the ideal opportunity to introduce empowerment in its purest form. There are no entrenched working practices to stand in the way; nobody to declare that the old way of doing things was far better. But the new Toyota plant at Burnaston in Derbyshire, where £19.2 million was spent on 100,000 man-hours of training even before production began in December 1992, illustrates that empowerment will only succeed if the ground has been carefully prepared in advance. As Bryan Jackson, the company's director of human resources and corporate affairs, puts it:

> People often say to me at Toyota UK how easy it must be to start with a greenfield site. But in truth we had just as big an opportunity to get it wrong as to get it right. We may well have a greenfield site but we have

'brownfield' employees.

Whether you are starting with a greenfield site or not, as well as building a new framework, you still have to remove existing frameworks. One of the frameworks that needs careful dismantling and then rebuilding is job description. At Toyota we are recruiting people as team members rather than selecting people against a job description.

As far as Toyota was concerned, previous car industry experience for the most part was irrelevant, but it did recruit against well-researched and defined criteria. Says Jackson:

> We wanted to find the right sort of people for Toyota – team players who would thrive in an atmosphere of trust and respect which encourages continuous improvement through empowerment.
>
> In some respects this was an advantage because addressing people's aptitude for flexibility and shared responsibility can be easier than trying to develop such aptitudes. After all, you also allow them to make an informed decision on whether it's right for them.

Toyota decided to give everyone who made an initial application a fair and equal opportunity to demonstrate their abilities. Quite a tall order considering the company had 20,000 applications for around a thousand jobs.

Part of the assessment included a job simulation exercise. For example, job applicants were asked to work together to produce fuel systems. They were put into teams but given complete freedom to organise themselves. Says Jackson:

> This gave us an idea of their ability to learn, work tempo, attention to detail and teamwork. It also gave candidates a fair idea of what it might be like working for Toyota. They were expected to produce top quality work to a certain pace, but they were given the opportunity to solve problems and improve their own team performance.

In Jackson's view, quality and empowerment march hand in hand. Sometimes this takes surprising forms:

> One lesson in our induction training, which highlights both trust and the number one goal of customer satisfaction, takes many new recruits by surprise. It is explained that never passing on a defect is fundamental to building in the quality customers expect. If any member is unable to pass

on good work, he pulls a cord suspended beside the line. Assistance is immediate, but the conveyor line will stop unless the problem can be solved.

In previous jobs all hell might have broken loose if a so-called shopfloor worker had stopped production. This is a very visible demonstration of not only our commitment to quality but also to empowering the individual.

A ROSE BY ANY OTHER NAME

There is still a lot of confusion about what empowerment really entails. David Bowen and Edward Lawler, two academics who have made a study of the issue, identify three distinct approaches which go under the guise of empowerment. The different approaches were referred to in an article by Christopher Lorenz in the 21 September 1992, issue of the *Financial Times*. The first is what the two academics call 'suggestion involvement', which is merely consultation dressed up as empowerment. It could be argued that McDonald's, the fast food chain uses this very limited form of 'empowerment'.

A second, more genuine, type of empowerment is what Bowen and Lawler call 'job involvement'. This entails extensive job re-design so that employees use a variety of skills, often in teams. They have considerable freedom in how they do the necessary work. Despite the increased empowerment that it brings, the job involvement approach does not change higher-level strategic decisions about organisation structure, power and the allocation of rewards. These remain senior management's responsibility.

A third level is what the two academics call 'high involvement' – a form practised by Federal Express and the Herman Miller furniture company in the United States. With 'high involvement', under Bowen and Lawler's definition, employees become involved not just in how to do their jobs, or how effectively their team performs, but also in the whole organisation's performance. Virtually every aspect of the organisation is different from that of a control-oriented one. Information on all aspects of the business performance is shared horizontally across the organisation, as well as up and down the –

usually delayered – structure. Employees develop extensive skills in teamwork, problem solving and business operations. They participate in work-unit management decisions. There is profit sharing and employee ownership.

HIGH PERFORMANCE

A good example of job involvement was the re-design of the administration department of Digital Equipment UK's north regional office in late 1989 to achieve high performance work flow. The administration of orders and contracts within the department had long been a source of widespread dissatisfaction, largely because it had grown in an *ad hoc* and uneven way over a large number of years. Attempts at local improvements had failed to address the real problem of increasing functionality and complexity. A design study was made to 'understand the part administration plays in the total order cycle and build the organisation to do that beautifully'.

The project team included representatives from each of the many groups involved in the old administration to ensure that all the knowledge required was available within the team. A diagonal slice approach ensured that all levels in the previous hierarchy were represented.

An early task was to define the work that was currently undertaken and map the administrative activity involved. It became apparent that every group was involved in virtually every stage of the transactional process. Managers and administrators formed two separate groups to define the 'ideal' flow of work and found, to their surprise, that they agreed. They also agreed on a definition of the purpose of administration, 'to turn orders into payable invoices'.

In designing the new organisation, the project team looked at five standard elements of work, people, structure, rewards and systems:

Work and people

These were considered together with the objective of *'designing the organisation and the jobs within it in such a way that people doing the work are motivated'*. By reviewing the causes of job satisfaction, it proved possible to ensure a coincidence of an individual's sense of purpose with that of the organisation. The project team decided that each administrator would take total responsibility for a balanced portfolio of accounts (range of sizes and complexity) and they would have the skills to perform all the (non-exceptional) administrative work necessary to support these accounts.

Structure

Groups of administrators would work close to internal and external customers in a flat organisation structure – all administrators would have equal status.

The role of manager was re-defined. Since the organisation would not be fragmented, the 'controlling' role of the manager would change to one of 'facilitating' – encouraging, coaching, enabling and nurturing the new organisation through its transition. The new organisation was sized at about forty per cent less than the former one.

Rewards

The new organisation had no status hierarchy on which pay could be mapped. A new pay system was designed which rewarded administrators for acquiring and applying skills and expertise which was seen to be valuable to the group.

Systems

The team recognised the need to change the unwieldy and uncoordinated nature of existing transaction processing systems. Enhancements and revisions were deferred until the new teams were working.

The overall vision was of a culture for continuous improvement where:

● the focus was on customer support with individuals taking ownership for the quality of their work,

- individuals continuously learned new skills and were rewarded for the application of those skills in doing their work,
- administrators would continually look for new ways of improving their processes and their output,
- managers supported their staff, coaching, enabling, then guiding them towards the vision.

Tangible results from implementing the new group included:

- reduction of staff from eighty-six to fifty-three
- reduction in managers from twelve to four
- volume throughput per administrator doubled
- salary bill reduced by almost thirty-five per cent
- ongoing cost savings of £560,000 per annum on salaries, £48,000 on office space.

Intangible results included improvements in process, quality of output, quality of working life and customer satisfaction.

BP'S FOUR BASIC RULES

Richard Newton, head of human resources at BP, has drawn up four basic rules for making empowerment effective, which he revealed at a conference on empowerment organised by *The Economist* in London in March 1993:

(1) *The need to articulate clearly and openly the company's business goals, both in the short term and of a more visionary nature.* The oil sector has been undergoing great change and will continue to do so. In such circumstances, honest, clear and non-patronising communication is vital. There must be a strong emphasis on face-to-face communication at every level. This takes time – management time, and time before the message sinks in and people really understand the business situation. But there are no short cuts. If you want people to rise to the challenge that empowerment presents, they must have a good knowledge and understanding of the issues their business faces.

(2) *Align individual aspirations with those of the company.* In other

words, reconcile career and personal objectives with business goals. Effectively answering the question 'if I deliver the performance the company wants, what's in it for me?' This is the most challenging aspect of the whole empowerment process. How do you tailor reward, recognition and development opportunities to encourage superior performance.

We describe this as *the yellow brick road* in which an individual's personal journey follows the same path as that of the business. But at some stage along the road, there can be a parting of the ways. And this need not be something to be feared. Indeed, all the training, self-development opportunities and rewards given to individuals in the past may increase their options outside the company. This is not a problem provided that the aims and objectives of both are consistent when it really matters.

The *yellow brick road* has, for sure, far-reaching implications. For example, not so long ago it was virtually unthinkable to discuss the possibility of resignation openly with your employer – unless you had already made up your mind to leave. It implied lack of commitment.

But in the new culture this is no longer the case. Some people clearly will spend their entire careers with a single company. Others won't want to – or won't be given the option. They may be more concerned, therefore, to develop their skills and experience with a view to moving on at a later date. In the new culture, aspirations need to be recognised and 'aligned' with the needs of the company itself.

This incidentally has far-reaching implications for companies too. There are likely in future to be many more 'comings and goings' with older and qualified people joining companies at more advanced stages of their career. This will have implications for career development within the company. It will also necessitate a very different kind of recruitment policy.

Alignment embraces many issues to do with training, self-development, rewards and recognition. Also, like business direction, it relies on effective communication and open, realistic two-way dialogue between a manager and his or her staff; a clear understanding of 'the rules of the game'.

(3) *Empowerment for BP is to recognise and encourage business*

flexibility or diversity. What works in Aberdeen won't necessarily work in Baglan Bay, let alone Baku, Bogota or Singapore. The watchword must be 'fit for purpose', with decisions taken as close to the local situation as possible. The centralised, global 'all singing, all dancing' models that we imposed in the past 'because they were best for everyone and therefore best for you' just don't work any more.

That is not to say, however, that any part of BP can afford to be 'an island'. We are a large, global, complex, multi-cultural organisation. One important source of competitive advantage is to benefit from experience and to ensure that different parts of the business learn from each other's activities.

(4) That's what I mean by a 'learning company'; and that is connected with my fourth and final empowerment rule. *If an organisation is to learn from its experiences, it must have effective global linkages in place.* Those linkages need not necessarily be of policy, but will also be of processes, networks – both formal and informal – and behaviour. The goal for us must be one of business flexibility *and* group synergy.

A DARK SIDE

Newton told his London audience that empowerment could be a great force for liberation – for enabling people to do things better and to tackle things in totally new ways. But it also needed to be a force for discipline; otherwise what starts out as democracy can end up in anarchy. 'There can be a dark side, which must be kept in check. Empowerment is about saying, "These are the business goals; these are the targets which must be met; this is the context and these are the processes within which we must operate. Use your own ingenuity, enterprise and initiative in achieving them."

SUMMARY

(1) The pressures for empowerment do not necessarily match the circumstances in which it is most likely to work appropriately. In

particular, the pressures for change are probably much more widespread than the circumstances in which empowerment will work. There is a very real risk that empowerment will be adopted in inappropriate circumstances, perhaps because it appeals to the values of those involved or because it is seen as a less painful way of bringing about change. When there are pressures for change but empowerment is inappropriate other solutions will be required. If organisations are in the wrong markets empowerment may be unable to resolve the problems. If there are too many tiers of management and too much central control self-managed work teams are unlikely to produce the savings necessary.

(2) The issue of control is central to the empowerment debate. As organisations grow in size more and more attention has focused on achieving consistency of approach, integration of efforts and minimisation of resources. These demands generate command and control organisations where managers see their tasks primarily in terms of planning, directing and controlling. These control systems are organisationally driven and based on feedback. Budgets are used to control expenditures but, once the budget is drawn up, the effective controls operate after the event. Appraisal systems rely on setting standards and targets which will deliver organisational goals and annual reviews to check progress. Such control systems share two fundamental weaknesses. They are owned by the organisation, not by the individuals concerned, and they relate to events which have occurred, not those which have yet to occur. Empowerment replaces these old control systems with personalised, individual feedforward control systems. In such systems staff anticipate difficulties before they arise and are able to resolve them before they develop. For such individual initiative to produce co-ordination, rather than anarchy, requires considerable congruity about goals and directions. The importance of this latter point was reflected in our research by those senior managers who emphasised the need for clarity about organisational missions and goals and business plans.

(3) The introduction of empowerment, for most organisations, is the equivalent of moving into the path of a gale. The organisation is exposed to forces far beyond its own strength. These forces may

enable the organisation to reach its destination far more quickly. Alternatively they may drive the organisation far from its course or even wreck it entirely if they are poorly handled. Among the issues to be considered in introducing empowerment are:

(i) Whether it is best introduced from the top down or from the bottom (middle) up? A Board level initiative announcing cultural change programmes to deliver an empowered learning organisation may attract much publicity. Some of it may even be favourable. It does not necessarily deliver empowerment to or from those who are currently disempowered. Launching an initiative in a particular plant with less fanfare but more resources may be far more appropriate. Lessons learned at one location can be transmitted if they are captured and understood. Empowerment requires a willingness to trust those at the front-line. Those at the front-line are most likely to believe they are trusted if they see changes in behaviour by their immediate managers. Anything else is spindrift – it looks dramatic but it adds nothing to the motion of the ship.

(ii) Can people be empowered against their will? Does empowerment come from within or without? If it is essentially an internal change, how can it be brought about by external agents? The short answers to these are 'no', 'within' and 'both'. More reasoned replies would include that people may initially be distrustful of empowerment but eventually choose to seize the opportunities available. Empowering experiences occur externally to the individual; they may be carefully orchestrated by the organisation. Including people in project teams gives them opportunities, and responding warmly to their suggestions may raise their confidence, but unless the results are internalised there will be no empowerment.

If the absence of empowerment is related to lack of skill or knowledge, to attitudes of low self-confidence (in the work setting) and powerlessness, then external change agents may offer development and opportunity and encouragement. If disempowerment reflects fundamental assumptions about the nature of society, about the gap between the powerful and the powerless, about self-worth and potential accomplishment, these barriers may prove too great for the most skilful of external agents. Such an employee might prefer to leave an empowered organisation for one which more appropriately matched his or her view of the world and place within it.

(iii) Some resistance to empowerment is inevitable. Some may come from those who feel threatened by it because their responsibilities will change (e.g. those managers and supervisors in closest contact with empowered groups). It may come from those whose views about the talents and capabilities of their staff do not admit the possibility that they could take over significant parts of the managerial role. It may also come from those whom it is sought to empower who, because of their conditioning or temperament, do not see empowerment as liberating. For all these groups the introduction of empowerment must be seen as the beginning of a change process to which there is considerable resistance. The change process must be managed accordingly.

(iv) Empowerment offers a radical challenge to the ways in which most organisations are managed. The first law of change states that one change leads to another. Empowerment, even if it is initially confined to defined areas and specific tasks, may raise expectations far beyond that. An empowerment process, once initiated, may produce levels of challenge not foreseen at its inception and not acceptable to powerful groups within the organisation. Empowerment poses tough questions about the nature, role and need for management. Empowerment may prove too radical for some organisations.

(v) Empowerment may be an appropriate response to particular sets of circumstances. What happens if those circumstances change? Suppose that empowerment is used to enable an organisation to deliver major changes in working practices to cope with a change in competitive pressure. Once the working practices have been altered it may be difficult to retain the same degree of enthusiasm for more routine tasks. Without further stimulus the impetus may decline in the face of routine and repetition. Such processes of decline may not be opposed by those managers who retain traditional concepts of organisation and management. At the same time such processes may be opposed by those who remain firmly committed to the values and advantages implicit in empowerment. It is unlikely that the shift from disempowerment to empowerment is a on–off switch any more than an individual's shift from ignorance to learning. It is more likely that it is a recurring option within processes of change – sometimes strong, sometimes weak, but rarely entirely absent.

At one level empowerment is not fundamentally different to other processes of change. Matching the current needs and circumstances of the organisation, being sensitive to its history and traditions, focusing on its strategic aims and objectives argues strongly that there is no single magic formula. Each organisation will adopt empowerment in its own way and some will be much more successful than others. The choices facing organisations include the level of intervention (e.g. corporate or plant), the style (e.g. conciliatory or aggressive), the foci (e.g. attitudes or behaviour), and the target for change (e.g. activities or results).

ACT OF FAITH

Management consultants Kinsley Lord, who have made a study of empowerment, recognise that a major effort is required to bring about a fundamental change of attitudes. Notes Stephen Taylor, the consultancy's chairman, 'The problem with building the empowered organisation is that it cannot be done by the methods of the command organisation. There is no continuous evolution towards it; it requires somewhere along the line an act of faith on the part of the management. It is a profound challenge to those who have built their careers by rising through the ranks of the command organisation.'

The empowered organisation, emphasises Kinsley Lord, is held together by forces different from those which bind the command organisation. 'If the conventional metaphor for the command organisation is a dinosaur, with the brain at the top issuing instructions to the ponderous body, then that of the empowered organisation might be a shoal of fish, moving rapidly and constantly adjusting its shape through signals that are instantly understood.'

To achieve that kind of organisational co-ordination requires managers and employees to inhabit a world that is alien to them both. Managers will have to learn to give up their former prerogatives of being the fountain of all wisdom and the master of all those they control. Employees will need to be convinced that management really believes in the new order and is not merely paying lip service to it. They will also have to seize the increased authority they are being given and use it in a way that falls well short of anarchy. They will have to believe in their abilities to have a greater say in their own future and greater control over their own destinies.

This is asking a great deal of both managers and staff. There will inevitably be resistance, born of fear and doubt, on both sides. Managers will often feel they are sacrificing their birthright, giving up power and losing control. Shopfloor workers will often be accused of joining the 'opposition' and betraying their fellow workers.

Nobody believes that these are easy changes to make. They require a lot of determination and faith, but the hope is that as the fruits of success become apparent more and more organisations will see the undeniable advantage of taking the empowerment route. Just how much of an adjustment needs to be made is examined in the next chapter which looks at the changed role of the manager.

Arguing that empowerment requires an act of faith may render it mystical for some. Being mystical may be more or less attractive to different managers. For many managers, bitter and joyous experience of their limited knowledge of cause and effect patterns in business and management render all major decisions (and many smaller ones) acts of faith. What is required for these managers to go forward are not miracles but only a reasonable belief that this avenue is preferable to others.

NUCLEAR ELECTRIC

Background

Under the original plans to privatise the electricity industry, the power stations were to be divided between two unequally sized companies, PowerGen and National Power, with the latter, larger company including what was then the nuclear arm of the Central Electricity Generating Board (CEGB). When it became clear that private sector investors were not willing to bear the heavy costs of decommissioning nuclear plants, the government was forced to reconsider. With few other options and time running out, nuclear power was withdrawn from the sale.

An eleventh-hour climb-down, though embarrassing, relieved the government of a major political headache. For those in the nuclear industry, however, it came as a severe blow, not least to their self-esteem. In the run-up to the intended sell-off, those in senior positions had been busy extolling the virtues of privatisation and developing an identity which would make them an integral part of National Power. Just a few months later those same managers had to explain to staff that they didn't quite make the grade and that privatisation wasn't such a good idea after all.

Thus it was that on 31 March 1990, with staff morale at an all-time low, Nuclear Electric plc was vested as a separate entity. Nuclear Electric was established as a separate limited company with one shareholder, the State. As Nick Hasell put it in a feature on Nuclear Electric in the July 1993 issue of *Management Today*: 'Despite the new name, the logo and the brave words, few – either inside or out – were wholly convinced. It was, to all effects, an unsaleable rump, a commercial oddity – a government-owned company in a competitive environment where all its competitors had been privatised.'

Ambitious targets

Despite this inauspicious start, Nuclear Electric has risen to the challenge. Although it did not make it to the private sector, Nuclear Electric has adopted the same sort of commercial approach as if it had. It has set itself ambitious targets to turn itself from a cost centre into a profit centre. Nuclear Electric's Hartlepool station, for example, set itself a target to go from a multi-million pound loss (when the government subsidy is excluded) to profit in three years. Since the government has put in place a system for steadily reducing its subsidy to the company, Nuclear Electric has little choice but to become more self-reliant. By 1993 the Hartlepool station had reduced its losses to £8 million and was confident that it would become profitable by 1994.

The Hartlepool station claims to have achieved this already considerable turnaround by empowering its employees. It has driven business planning down into the heart of the organisation and has introduced a concept of teamworking that has revolutionised former entrenched working practices. True to the best practices of empowerment it went to the workers themselves to explore the best forms of teamwork. The approach was not without its difficulties since engineers have always been the top dogs in nuclear power stations and they did not always take kindly to the idea of having to take a back seat in some of the cross-functional teams set up under the new approach.

It was found that it was pointless just tinkering with existing work teams since these were often dealing with a fragmented part of the whole work process, which limited their scope of action. Process re-engineering was therefore introduced with the help of socio-technical analysis, a technique that looks at both the technical and the people side of work processes.

When a team was set up to try to streamline the process by which the fuel rods are routed through the reactor, it was found there was over-manning and that simple tasks were being undertaken by skilled engineers. This has resulted in multi-skilling (or skill broadening as Nuclear Electric prefers to call it). While craftsmen still retain their core skills, it has been agreed that peripheral skills can be shared among other team members.

Work improvement groups looking at such areas as safety and energy efficiency have also scored some major successes. In 1992, the 'outage' – the period when a reactor is closed down for maintenance – was reduced from sixteen to ten weeks after a team was set up to explore ways of simplifying the procedures. This has saved millions of pounds by increasing significantly the amount of power generated.

The eight-strong Change Support Team (CST) which is spearheading the new approach at Hartlepool, is steadily taking more of a back seat role as the programme takes hold. It sees its main function as providing the tools by which the work teams can forge their own progress, now that the necessary infrastructure is in place. The support team now primarily provides training and consultancy services to the empowered work teams, which set out their own change strategy in their business plans.

Hartlepool, which bench-marked other electrical power stations in Sweden and the US, as well as a number of 'empowered' companies in the UK, chose not to use Total Quality Management (TQM) as its change catalyst. Ian Briggs, the station's change agent, argues that it is necessary to achieve 'quantum leaps' in a major change programme before TQM can hope to be successful. TQM, he maintains, progresses in painstaking incremental steps that are insufficiently dramatic to inspire the fundamental changes of style necessary to steer an organisation like Nuclear Electric in radically new directions. He believes it is better first to find ways to enable the work teams to 'own' the change programme and that TQM can then be built on the back of that.

Vanguard of change

When Tony Capp took over as station manager at Hartlepool in June 1991 the decision had already been taken to introduce a culture change programme to take account of its new situation. It was a challenge that Capp relished and he was resolved to put Hartlepool in the vanguard of the change programme necessary to transform Nuclear Electric's fleet of twelve power stations. But he didn't underestimate the task before him or the outmoded command and control management system that he had inherited. He recalls:

> We had all the normal controls of nationalised industries – heavily bureaucratic, strictly run by government. The local manager was just

given lots of targets. He was given little pots of money to pay salary bills, for example, with no real power to move money around against what he saw as the business objectives. That was no different from any other nationalised industry.

But the electricity generating industry was saddled with an additional handicap. Explains Capp, 'The perceived problem with the CEGB was that it had a statutory obligation to supply energy. If you wanted a supply, we had to supply you, whether or not it was cost-effective. We were a cost centre. So long as at the end of the year I could account for everything I had spent, that was all I was really account-able for.'

One of Capp's first actions after taking charge was to examine the exact nature of the change programme that was required. The main impetus for change at Hartlepool, operating in the cold, harsh world of private enterprise was a very stark one. If it didn't change its culture it was quite possible that it would not be around much longer. 'We had a very big business threat that if we didn't improve our profitability it was quite possible our industry wouldn't survive,' Capp puts in bluntly.

There was considerable evidence to suggest, however, that the nuclear energy industry could operate at a profit. Government reviews had already concluded that the industry could be made viable. Hartlepool is well on the way to demonstrating that this positive view of the industry's prospects can be substantiated. In its financial year ending 31 March 1993, it reduced the previous year's losses of £71 million (discounting the government levy) to a mere £8 million loss.

Declares Capp proudly, 'That's an enormous step to make in one go. The year we are in now we are determined we shall actually be cash positive. All the markets are there. We just have to do the business now.'

No golden right

Achieving this remarkable turnaround has required some funda-mental changes of attitude at the Hartlepool station. Says Capp:

I had to turn the culture around from a cost-based accountancy system to a profit-based system and we have had to instill in people that we are a business. We are not here as a public legacy; we are not here with a golden right to be here as long as we want; we are not an experiment; we are a business. If we don't make ourselves profitable, then we won't survive.

The main thrust of the change programme is

to make the staff own the problem. That has meant awakening all the latent talent. We believe that a lot of the 720 staff are highly talented individuals. Many of them have quite challenging interests outside work, such as running a yacht club. To give you another example, we have a team that in their spare time are very enthusiastic about dragon boat racing (a sport that is very popular in the Far East). From a standing start, they've become the English champions and two years ago went to Hong Kong to represent the UK.

In other words, outside the gates they're motivated; they organise; they budget, whether they're running scout groups or raising money for charity.

If the change programme was to succeed, Capp realised that he needed to open up communication channels with the staff. A survey was carried out to find out exactly what the staff thought about the company. Capp made a number of presentations as part of the awakening process to familiarise everyone at the plant with the task confronting them. He has followed this up with quarterly meetings at which all the staff at Hartlepool are given an overview of the current state of the business. Adds Capp, 'We go into the major accounts; we show them what the cash flow is; what the threat is. I treat them as shareholders. This is all part of the communication, showing them that there is a problem, but also how we can become profitable, because there are a number of sceptics on the staff.'

Trial and error

Capp admits that he did not have any preconceived notion of how to bring about the necessary culture change and that there has been a lot of trial and error along the road. As he puts it:

you start off with a dream and you find out what the problems are as you go along. We've had to overcome an enormous number of hurdles and we've still got a long way to go. Many of the shopfloor workers, for want of a better word, are now motivated. Many of them understand what the business is about and many of them feel that they can contribute to that and regularly do so.

At the top, quite a number of the departmental heads are motivated about the change. But we have a tranche in the middle who are less easily won over. It's the middle group we are having trouble with. Traditionally, all companies have had the same problem. Status is a huge problem. So we are using the bottom to come up and we've got the top pushing down.

To put everyone's mind at rest, Capp pledged at the outset that there would be no compulsory redundancies as a result of the change programme. He admits, 'This is a shackle around our legs because you are not able to decide who are the key players and who are the non-key players and get rid of the non-key and recruit new key workers. So we're going about this revolution in a fairly quiet way, chipping away at the problems all the time.'

Reservoir of specialists

Staff who are uncomfortable with the new culture are being pulled out of the core operations and put into a reservoir of specialist talent for training and development and to become members of special project groups. There was a real danger that these people would regard such deployment as the thin end of the wedge and that they would be the first to go if management broke its pledge and dismissed people as part of the downsizing programme. But Capp claims that such fears have been put to rest:

There are good examples of people who are very motivated by these projects which are a big cultural change in themselves. We've got some people who are real blockers in the new culture, but who have taken to the training initiative like a duck to water. The key issue is we're not pulling people out and putting them into these other tasks because they've got no contribution to make. We're actually leaving some of the non-players ticking over in their jobs while we take the real players and use them to drive forward change.

The change programme has meant looking closely at the way work is performed at Hartlepool and in particular at whether engineers, who have traditionally dominated the nuclear energy industry, are being deployed to the best advantage.

We have highly-skilled professional staff doing manual jobs because of the way the work has developed. They are doing work which in other industries and in nuclear power stations in other countries are undertaken by hourly paid staff. In France, for example, the control room of nuclear power stations is manned by hourly staff.

We have graduate engineers actually getting involved with the nuts and bolts of maintenance. We have got all this skill and investment in them: we actually want to develop that professionalism; we actually want to use them for what they're good at. That's empowerment. We're trying to soften the threat by looking at the skills necesssary to undertake certain processes and asking how the skills can be shared. It's a learning curve for them. Some of them try to hang on to the way it has always been done because they're frightened of losing status or even their jobs.

Change is difficult to measure, but Capp likens it to a liner during a cruise.

You're looking at the horizon all the time. It's only when you look back and see the wake of the boat that you realise you have shifted twenty or thirty degrees. We're the same. The change programme and our investment in people is quite considerable, but I think we're towards the end of the investment phase now; we're seeing the results. We increased the output from the station last year (1992/93) by forty per cent. Our income has increased by £70 million and at the same time we've reduced the work force by fifty people.

Productivity

The staff reductions have been achieved through voluntary redundancy, but when Capp first put forward the idea that the station could be made more profitable with less staff there were many who thought it could not be done, since the view was that the station was already working flat out. However, when he asked people to estimate the productivity of the average person at the station nobody could put it higher than fifty per cent of what it could be. Capp reasoned that by improving that marginally to seventy-five per cent, it would release 350 people a year.

> It was clear that the staffing level was not the problem; it was the way that people were working that needed to be tackled. So we have allowed fifty to go (voluntary redundancy), which has reduced the salary bill. And we have twenty people – progressively increasing – who have been pulled out of the core operations looking at new computer management systems for budgeting and similar projects.

In addition, Hartlepool's work load has increased as a result of Nuclear Electric's decision to decentralise some of the staff functions that were previously managed from head office. The personnel function, for example, has been devolved to the local stations.

> Under the previous setup station managers had very little power to appoint people. I now appoint everybody and my own personnel staff deals with them. In the past devolution equalled more people. Now we increase the productivity of the existing staff.
>
> To start with it's an act of faith. Now I've got less people in personnel doing a bigger job more effectively and enjoying it more because now they can turn their attention to strategic matters. They used to pay people, but I've now moved wages to another group on the station.

Pioneer

Pioneering a change programme in itself adds to the work load, as Capp points out, 'I'm going to be the first one constantly knocking up against problems – problems of culture, problems of how to pay people, how to assess people's competence and introduce competency-based systems. I can only attend to all of that if people are taking over the other areas from me. So it forces me and my colleagues into looking at the way we work.'

Hierarchy

Capp inherited a typical hierarchical management structure when he took charge at Hartlepool. The station manager's top management team consisted of managers in charge of production, engineering, administration and resources. The administration manager dealt with finance because as a cost centre the station was merely expected to account for its expenditure. Between them and the shopfloor there were eight layers of management. 'How do you communicate through eight layers?'

Capp introduced a new structure, which reduced the management layers, but at the same time spread the responsibilities more widely. For example, he hired a professional accountant, which the station had never had before. 'Last year (1992/93) we had a turnover of £324 million and we didn't have a station accountant. You had somebody in charge of wages, somebody looking at procurement and those sorts of things. Now we have a professional accountant.'

Business planning

Once Hartlepool recognised what the main sticking points to culture change were and had restructured the organisation it was in a better position to set goals for the future. 'We realised that the major culture change had to be hung completely and squarely on the business. Culture change for us is about the business plan,' says Capp.

The business plan in the CEGB days was put together by the station manager and his head of resources. At one of the workshops Capp ran to seek ideas from selected groups of managers, the observation was made that managers never had sight of the station's business plan. The complaint was: 'we don't know what the targets are for the station, for example. You keep the salary budgets squarely locked up in your top drawer because you don't want us to know how much is paid out in salary and overtime and all those vexed questions.'

Capp found the complaint to be absolutely justified. There were four or five copies of the plan that were kept secret on a 'need-to-know' basis.

Price Waterhouse was brought in for a month to advise the Hartlepool station on how to introduce comprehensive business planning and to help train those members of the staff who, as Capp calls them, are 'budget-holders'. These are not exclusively managers. The person who runs the station's information centre, for example, is not a manager but is a budget-holder.

> We already had many budget-holders, but all they knew was what their budget was and they only knew as much of their budget as they needed to know. We've changed all that.
>
> The introduction of the business planning process has been a remarkable change for the station. It's the first leg of getting real ownership, of not just handling and accounting for your budget, but actually having a say in what your budget should be.

The planning process has been simplified to address two basic issues: what does the budget-holder want in terms of resources and what is he or she going to deliver. The budget-holders are measured against what they promise to deliver in return for the resources they have been given.

Capp admits that the planning process is still far from perfect:

> but it's beginning to shake down, because I've involved them in a tough set of negotiations. Equally, it's made my job much more challenging, because I now have to sit down and decide what I want. Before they can put in their business plan, I have to tell them what the objectives are. In the past I would tell the production manager that I wanted all he could deliver without defining it. Now I have to agree with him what his annual budget is based on – delivering so many terrawatts of energy. He now has to work out how he is going to manage all the various components.

Outage

Capp sees top management playing a progressively less directive role in day-to-day operations and increasingly playing the role of coach and adviser. He claims he is working towards the idea of self-managed work groups which act semi-autonomously. He cites the team set up to reduce the 'outage', the period of time the reactor is out of commission while maintenance and repairs are carried out:

> Last year I took my hand off the outage. I set the objective by saying: 'Outages take too long. Let's have a look at the problem.' Then I let it be known that I was prepared to take my hand off the handle – but making it clear what they had to deliver. I set aside a budget of £3.2 million to do the work. I also indicated that it would be worker-led and that we would

invest in some novel ways of finding the solution. I wanted the outage done in twelve weeks (rather than the normal sixteen weeks). That was the challenge.

The budget for the outage was precisely what it had been the previous year, which was Capp's way of saying that the problem would not be solved by throwing money at it. The team set up to investigate the outage went to Sweden to examine how the problem was tackled there. They were not interested in technical issues, but in 'soft' issues, such as how teams are organised in Sweden and how they communicate.

As a result of this research the team found ways to complete the outage within ten weeks, beating Capp's own target by two weeks. Since every day the reactor is out of commission, the station loses £300,000 in lost energy production, this was a very considerable saving. Some £350,000 was saved by hiring in temporary skilled labour and reducing the amount put out to contract. It also meant the outage team could have more control over the maintenance operations. Such is the availability of skilled staff on the unemployment register in the Teesside area there was little difficulty in finding people of the right calibre.

Capp is still not satisfied. He believes the outage can be brought back to nine weeks, if a special effort is made. Next time around there will be the added incentive of a bonus for those involved if they manage to achieve the work in record time.

Driving force

Capp sees empowerment as the driving force of the change programme at Hartlepool. 'In our definition of empowerment we are not abdicating management accountability or responsibility. Managers are here to set targets with the involvement of the staff. Whereas in the past I would be involved in every technical issue, I now merely set wider targets.'

Capp sees empowerment as the means to achieve three main business goals – profitability, improved safety standards and public awareness.

We have to be a profitable station; otherwise we won't survive – but not at any cost. If we don't have high safety standards we will be shut down anyway. The two go hand in hand. The final factor is public awareness.

Even if you drive hard on your economics and on your safety you still have problems if you haven't won over public awareness, as we saw in the coal debate. The government is driven by public awareness. We have made a big investment in an information centre.

We're investing in safety by highlighting it as a separate department and bringing together lots of diverse issues which were dotted around different management's accountability.

New direction

Achieving change at Hartlepool has sometimes been a slow and painstaking business, as Capp admits:

The first year was spent slowing down the old culture and pointing the organisation in the new direction. We've slowed it to a stop. We're slowly but surely putting the effort into winding it up again and finding all the classical change symptoms. A nuclear power station is no different to any other business.

There were lots of arguments, because when you start to empower people you have to be able to deal with the negative side as well. It's the negative ones that drive you downhill. They wanted money before change. 'If this is all about improving business performance, we want a share of it.' (To offset this complaint the Hartlepool station has introduced a gainsharing programme.)

We have had some bun fights and we got to the bottom, but we are on the upslope now. Every now and again we have a hiccup and slide back down a bit. As you get the improved productivity, that releases staff you can then invest in the change programme.

Causing pain

It has been spelled out to budget-holders that the change programme is not just an add-on process. They are now required to deliver their plan for change as part of their business plan. The station departments are starting to appoint their own change agents to drive the programme. The engineering department, for example, has appointed a reactor physicist, a young high-flyer. It was an agonising decision to release such a key member of staff from the core business. Says Capp:

> The engineering manager was having difficulty because he worked out that the right people to become change agents were all people he couldn't afford to lose and I said: 'In the end, can you afford not to? Unless you choose the right calibre of individual you aren't going to make progress.'
>
> One of the things I learned from a fact-finding visit to America is that if it isn't causing you pain, you've made the wrong choice.

(NB: In July 1993 Nuclear Electric as a whole significantly improved its financial performance announcing an increase in annual profits. They climbed to £109 million in the year to 31 March from £62 million in the previous twelve months after paying for redundancies and financing charges.

Chairman John Collier said, 'I can see Nuclear Electric carrying its commercial success through to the point where a move out of the state sector is recognised as feasible and desirable. This would then complete the privatisation of the electricity supply industry in England and Wales.'

Nuclear Electric receives a reducing annual subsidy of £1.3 billion from consumers, known as the non-fossil fuel levy, which is intended to run out in 1998. Without the levy the company would make losses. However, Collier expects Nuclear Electric to be profitable without the levy by 1995–96.

Sales of electricity increased during the year to £1.4 billion and output rose by 14 per cent. Productivity per employee increased by 23 per cent, while unit costs of electricity fell by 11 per cent and market share rose 21.6 per cent.)

Comment

A nuclear power station may seem an unlikely setting for a transformation through empowerment. It evidently does not meet some of the criteria we indicated as being particularly important in Chapter One. As electricity is a commodity which, in Britain, Nuclear Electric sells through the 'pool', station staff have little chance to get close to their external customers. Much of the work on a power station is routine and repetitive. Sections of the management and the workforce were less than totally enthusiastic about the changes.

Yet Hartlepool has made enormous progress. The improvements in financial and production performance are obvious. Less obvious but no less real is the change in staff attitudes and behaviour. Not only did the staff meet Capp's targets for outage reduction, they exceeded them. That suggests a degree of self-confidence and a sense of commercial competitiveness which were not evident in the old culture. Responsiveness to 'internal' customers through project teams has jumped.

Key factors in moving the process forward clearly include the degree of external change through privatisation of the other generators and the new arrangements for the sale of electricity, the fear of an increasingly unstable environment with new generators entering the market, the commitment of Capp and other senior managers at Hartlepool and elsewhere in Nuclear Electric, and the willingness of staff at all levels to try new ways of thinking and new ways of working. Capp has invested heavily in upgrading staff skills through business planning and skill broadening.

Some significant issues remain. The major strides appear to have been made in the non-routine areas of work (e.g. outages and introduction of new systems). It appears easier to generate enthusiasm and action for empowerment around non-routine activities. Senior management are still in the role of determining the targets and largely driving the change process. Capp states 'we actually want to use them for what they're good at. That's cmpowerment.' This statement simultaneously recognises the latent talent of the work force and reserves to management the right of direction. Self-managed work teams have been primarily focused on 'how things should be done, rather than 'what things should be done'. Coaching emerges more strongly as a realisation that the old command and control systems no longer function effectively than as a fully articulated change of management approach and behaviour. The investment in staff development is described in terms of a one-off investment which, having been completed, can now be reaped, rather than an on-going process of adaptation.

BP EXPLORATION (BPEX)

The prospect of declining productivity from its major oil fields in the North Sea and at Prudhoe Bay in Alaska proved to be the spur for empowerment at BP Exploration (BPEX). Says Tom Standing, head of organisational development for BPEX:

> Every organisation has to come face to face with some real crisis before it gets the resolve to do anything that is different from what it has done historically. You need that sense of urgency and sudden rise in dissatisfaction with where you are now. For the North Sea and for Prudhoe Bay it was the reality of the decline in oil production. Each of them were huge, marvellous fields, but each has a life span and it happens, either to our regret or our opportunity, that both those fields are declining at the same time.

BP's response to this daunting challenge was to empower its oil production workers to contribute ideas on how they could extend the economic life of both these major fields. The effort was launched in 1991 with a programme called Operation Bridge to draw up a plan of how the oil fields' productive life could be prolonged to the year 2010.

To measure the enormity of the task, a picture was painted of the difference between the oil fields at their peak and what could be expected to happen to them in the immediate future. Says Standing, 'the future was a picture of much smaller oil fields, much lower volumes of production from a lot of different fields, much tighter control requirements on costs, much more creativity on how we use the technology.'

There would be a shift from a few huge producing fields to a situation where there would have to be the same level of production (around 500,000 barrels a day), but from a very different operation and very different constraints on it in terms of business requirements. Adds Standing, 'That set the context for people in the operations to say: "if that's the challenge, how do I meet it?" It energised everyone right down to the operators on the platform and it was a lot to do with communicating business reality to people.'

Standing contends that BP management had little choice but to put the oil workers fully in the picture even if it meant that the motivation to take drastic steps was based on fear, an emotion that is hardly compatible with empowerment:

> Fear may be the reaction, but you can't deny that if you don't get better profitability the fields will be shut down. So do you sit in the executive suite and say: 'Boy, this is terrible. I guess we had better plan to close those platforms', or do you actually go out to the work force, as a sort of coach, and say 'We see the bigger playing field; you're down there head to head with your competitor; we can see that there's only two minutes left to play in this game, we thought you'd like to know that the whistle is going to blow in two or three years'?
>
> It was facing people with the reality of the job situation. Let's see what we can do to extend the life of the fields by reducing costs, including efficiency of the operation, using technology more cleverly. Or, if we can do that for only so long, how do we actually carry on our employment in other areas, either in these developing fields or in other parts of the UK?

The size of the challenge is evident from some startling statistics. Every 110,000 barrels of liquid that is pumped out of the North Sea today produces a mere 10,000 barrels of oil. The rest is water. That is because the field has been operating for around thirteen years and as the oil is extracted sea water fills the vacuum. Originally the field was producing 109,000 barrels of oil for every 110,000 barrels of liquid extracted. The hard economics of that decline in productivity is that it now costs as much to produce 10,000 barrels of oil as it did 109,000. The only way to close that gap is to find innovative ways to bring down costs.

BPEX set up special study teams and organised off-site meetings with its staff to generate suggestions on how the fields could be run at lower costs. But before the oil workers could be expected to contribute ideas, BP recognised that they had to be a lot better informed than had previously been the case about the fundamentals of what made the business tick. Says Standing:

> It meant giving people a lot more information than they had before about production costs, about sources of value and losses of value in the field – where we were spending money, what would help in terms of spending some of the maintenance money over a longer period of time or handling

shutdowns in ways that reduced the amount of time the field was out of commission, so that the production level for that year would be higher.

All sorts of ideas were brought out of the organisation and that virtually is the fundamental idea of empowerment. We were putting into operation this notion that with every pair of hands you get a free brain. How do you get the brain engaged along with the hands?

BPEX pulled no punches in making the oil workers aware of their future prospects and how vital it was for them to play their part in coming up with solutions. They did not even flinch from admitting that the operators could well be developing plans that would lead to their own departure. Says Standing:

Operators at the bottom level were being told that we really did need their ideas, but that there was going to be fewer of them. We appealed to them to help us plan how we would get to the point where the few that were left would feel very good about what they were doing and those who would depart would feel good about what they were leaving behind.

It's this idea: if you know you are going to die, don't you want to do it with some dignity? It may look a bit like using fear as a prod, but I think it is using reality. A lot of the paternalistic orientation of oil companies has been that it is too scary for the folks down there, so we won't tell them about it and then the day you close the plant, you tell them. Is that really helping them get over their fear?

Fully in the picture, the empowered teams tackled the complex issue of extending the life span of declining oil fields in a variety of ways. In Alaska, for example, they introduced what is now known as process re-engineering, but which was known simply as process improvement when BP took it up. Simplifying processes has led to considerable cost reductions. In 1987 BPEX's Alaska operation was staffed by 1,500 people. Today the manning level has dropped to below 1,000 while maintaining the same production levels.

Total productive maintenance

Forties Alpha, one of BP's North Sea platforms, has introduced the technique of total productive maintenance (TPM), something that had never before been attempted on an offshore installation. TPM is not a new concept. It has been used successfuly in Japanese industry for over 20 years. The dual goal of TPM is zero breakdowns and zero defects, thereby reducing costs and increasing labour productivity. Some Japanese companies that have introduced major TPM programmes have seen a ninety per cent reduction in process defects and a general increase in labour productivity of forty to fifty per cent.

For BP it was a new way of working. It meant breaking down barriers that had been established over the years. It changed its working practices from single discipline based activities to teamwork, focusing on what was best for the asset. Everyone from managers to deck operators had an important role to play. Old taboos were laid to rest in the drive for excellence.

Initially, BP decided on a pilot project that satisfied key conditions: everyone had to be involved, it would have to have a positive effect on profitability, and lessons had to be learned that could be applied more generally. With those conditions in mind, it was decided to target the produced water disposal system (PWD). This was a major challenge because of the negative effect it was having on overall efficiency and the ability to produce maximum oil.

An extensive training programme was undertaken to familiarise the operations teams (onshore and offshore) with the TPM system. Facilitators were trained to assist the teams and co-ordinate the project. Throughout the project milestones were set to measure progress and to ensure that direction and a sense of purpose were maintained.

The initial benefits delivered from the project were increased teamwork, plant familiarisation and the sharing of experience. For the first time many operators and technicians started to have a say in plant optimisation and began to have an understanding about equipment effectiveness and operating costs. A system and formula were worked out to measure the equipment effectiveness and to resolve issues that had an undue effect on its performance.

A progress report on the success of BP's approach to TPM was presented to the Offshore Europe conference staged by the Society of Petroleum Engineers at Aberdeen in September 1993. The report was prepared by Les Thomson, a BP offshore installation manager, and members of the empowered teams working on the Forties Alpha platform. It was probably the first time such a paper had ever been jointly prepared by technicians and supervisors on a production platform for a major oil conference, which in itself was an indication of BP's commitment to empowerment:

Everything that we attempted did not come off and we struggled at times to see the benefits. It was costing us both time and money to return the plant to its original condition and to address some of the major issues. We also struggled with understanding our new style independence, but generally thrived on the challenge. The biggest percentage of the suggested improvements were simple maintenance activities that were incorporated into our weekly work plan. Other, more technical, problems were passed to our extended team onshore and their expertise was invaluable in solving some major problems.

We were developing into a single focused unit with a desire to succeed. All our problems as yet have not been solved, but generally speaking, we have had a positive response from everyone we have approached. The final challenge is to move from an independent approach to full interdependence across the team, between onshore and offshore, and with partners and customers – the final stages of adolescence into adulthood.

A sense of job ownership

To Thomson and his team empowerment means:

creating a sense of job ownership by giving clear direction, having control of resources, real responsibility and appropriate coaching; it means offering help without removing responsibility. In practice that necessitates leaders establishing clear goals and expectations, as well as providing the tools to complete the task. It means encouragement, trust, integrity, recognition that our associates are an integral part of our day to day lives, and listening and responding to their and others' needs with respect and empathy.

Fifty cents a barrel

A more general target to inspire BP's empowered oil workers was set by John Browne, chief executive of BPEX, who identified strongly with the Project 90 culture change programme introduced by Bob Horton, BP's former chairman. Browne set an across-the-board target in 1991 to increase the profit margin on a barrel of oil by fifty cents – a rise of twenty per cent to be found out of improved efficiency and cost cutting. He originally set the target to be achieved over a three year time period, but as it became apparent that BP was hitting hard times and its profitability was less than anticipated, he shortened the deadline to two years. The target was met by the end of 1992. Says Standing:

> There's something about having clear goals that are measurable and difficult to achieve that energises people. It's the same in sport. Going after a record is a very good motivator. Often in business the yardsticks are so removed from the operating level and so convoluted that they don't provide motivation. The fifty cents a barrel target was a tool management throughout the organisation could talk about to the production workers, to the geologist, to the reservoir engineer and it got them thinking about net income.

The message that came from the exercise was that to improve profitability and extend the life of declining oil fields the focus had to be on cost cutting. It was impossible to control price. That was set by the world market, largely by OPEC. Volume, which is the other ingredient in profit, is set mainly by the capacity of the drilling equipment and the size of the oil field. That takes time to change. The only element that everyone in the business can influence is overhead cost. Says Standing, 'it's price minus cost times volume equals profit. That was a very simple message that everyone throughout the organisation could understand. We do have to worry about profitability and we therefore do have to worry about costs. It's the only element of the equation we can control.'

Surprise?

So has BP been pleasantly surprised by the ingenuity of its empowered oil operators?

> I wouldn't say pleasantly surprised because in the upstream business we have always had a healthy respect for the capability right down into the

organisation and some of it is attributable to high standards of recruitment, including blue collar hiring, and the development of people for the platforms. But what we have found is that they can be stretched much further than maybe we thought they could in being inventive about how to run a production operation. There's some very sharp people who have chosen to go into relatively manual work because they like machinery, they like equipment. They are very good at thinking about how you can run it and when you get into the electronics and control side, it brings out all sorts of things that people are good at which you may not have known about.

I hate to say pleasantly surprised because it suggests we thought they were a bunch of dummies and it turns out they weren't. I don't think we ever felt that way. I just think there was a lot of bureaucracy that inhibited managers from providing the sort of latitude which showed where people could get to if you gave them a chance. A lot of it was about control. We were a very control-oriented business; a lot of hierarchy; a lot of the power of the office.

Comment

Among the most noticeable features of the BP experience is the extent to which emotion reveals itself as a driving force in change. In their approach to acknowledging the problems and the required solutions BP talk about having to use fear as a means of motivation. The fear of losing jobs, the fear of watching operations close are very real. But their account misses the excitement which is generated when people are afraid. It misses the adrenalin rush which is created by fear and the knowledge that you can do something about it. In explaining the BP experience it seems likely that the strong performance of platform workers was not simply a product of fear or of the considerable talents but also of the excitement they felt in being involved in matters from which they were previously excluded.

Another strong feature of the BP experience is the benefit of having clear and powerful performance measures. These are not necessarily the same as targets – partly because in radical change it is not always clear what is the right direction, but it is important to measure progress. BP were able to combine targets and performance measures in a way which gave clear direction to the efforts of the empowered workforce.

There was less emphasis in the BPEX case on the need to re-skill and develop their workforce. There was considerable emphasis on the need to explain the whole position fully to the workforce and make them acquainted with the position facing the organisation.

BPEX and Nuclear Electric at Hartlepool shared the approach of being much more open with the workforce about the business position confronting them. In both cases the organisations have already made their major investment and are now concerned with maximising the yield from that investment. In both cases work patterns involve a good deal of routine and repetition and meticulous attention to safety. The conditions for empowerment are not ideal but both seem to have made real progress.

3

THE CHANGING ROLE
OF THE MANAGER

If the traditional role of the manager has always been to plan, organise, direct and control, what is there left for him to do when he hands all this over to an empowered work force or a self-managed work group? By endorsing the trend to empowerment, is he in fact ringing his own death knell? This is undoubtedly the fear in the minds of many managers who resist the encroachment of empowerment and are reluctant to relinquish power. But it is not an issue that troubles Roy Page, production supervisor at Minicraft, an autonomous business unit attached to Black and Decker's accessories division at Pennymoor in the North East of England.

Page's working life has changed dramatically in the course of a year and he is relishing every moment of it. 'I have wanted this something terrible!' he declares, which might sound a strange reaction from someone who has virtually handed over control to the shopfloor workers he used to command with all the authority of his superior rank.

The reason for Page's change of heart is the introduction of cell manufacturing at Minicraft which has brought about a switch from process-based batch production (Fig. 3.1) to product-based single unit manufacture (Fig. 3.2). Each of the six low voltage power tools produced at the Spennymoor factory for hobbyists and DIY enthusiasts has its own manufacturing unit run by a dedicated group of assembly workers.

Under the old system Page worked late into the night and often over the weekend trying to organise the production flow to make the maximum use of the work force. There were often long delays in fulfilling orders because the quantities required were insufficient to

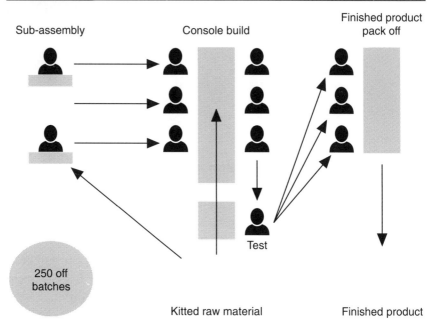

Fig. 3.1   Process-based batch production

justify re-tooling the assembly line. The introduction of cell production has brought an end to Page's nightmare. Not only can he cope with small production runs; he has also handed over almost total responsibility to the women on the shopfloor for meeting customer targets.

'It's now up to the people out there, the people who are actually working on the shopfloor,' he says with considerable relief. 'What they want we try to give them. We (management) are just here to support them. The role has changed from them supporting us to us now supporting them. If they want something we've got to support them. That's our main purpose in life.'

This is the inverted pyramid in practice. Focusing on the need to

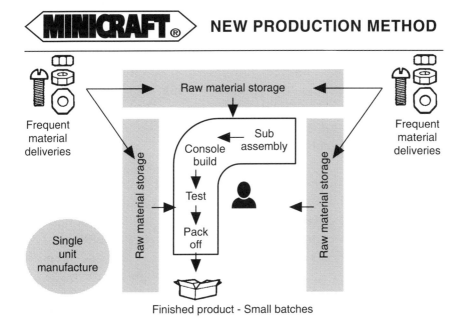

Fig. 3.2   Product-based single unit manufacture

meet customer demands involves elevating the importance of those best able to meet those demands. It is not too fanciful to see a parallel between the attitude to customers and that to the workforce. Under the old system customers were told they had to wait until there were sufficient orders – a version of command and control. A more customer-focused approach – meeting customer orders when the customer wants – leads to a more hands-off management style to enable the work force to respond to customer needs.

DRIVING FORCE

The driving force behind the new approach at Minicraft is Francis Barnish, the operations manager, a strong advocate of empowerment with the determination to see it put into practice. When he took over the small-scale Minicraft operation he saw it as an ideal opportunity to implement some of the empowerment theories he strongly believed in. His resolve to make empowerment work is making a lot of people happy at Spennymoor. Page now leaves the office on time and is free to spend his weekends on social activities. The assembly workers talk enthusiastically about 'owning' their own production cells and enjoying the satisfaction of making the tools from start to finish rather than merely making sub-assemblies as was the case on the old conventional product line.

Each product cell is 'owned' by two assembly workers. Their priority is to make sure their cell is operating to capacity whenever there are orders. If the orders run out for their particular product line they go and help out at one of the cells that is working flat out. That is virtually the only time they consult Page. As co-ordinator, he tells them where their services are most needed, but while they are working in their own cell they run their own affairs and the result has been that they have consistently met or exceeded production targets, whereas previously they invariably fell well short.

Because they now assemble complete products and pack them ready for despatch, the shopfloor workers are also becoming multi-skilled. 'They've all been trained so that they can actually go into any cell. If somebody is off sick it's no longer a problem. Someone whose cell is not running covers for the person who has not turned up,' explains Page.

The shopfloor workers were involved in devising the new method of working from the start and they run regular meetings to discuss problems or new ideas of making the system run even more smoothly. They invite managers to the meetings, but the managers are simply there to provide any necessary information and to offer their support. If they are requested to attend a meeting they are obliged to go, but they cannot insist on taking part if the shopfloor workers see no reason for their presence.

TRANSFORMATION

The shopfloor workers, like Page, can hardly believe the trans-formation that has taken place in their lives. Not so long ago the only influence they had on the products they assembled was a cost saving suggestion box scheme. Their ideas were hardly ever taken up by management because each idea in itself rarely amounted to a significant enough financial saving. Management regarded few of the suggestions worth implementing.

In addition, the engineers who regarded it as their job to come up with innovative ideas resented shopfloor workers usurping their role even though the people closest to the problem are the most likely to see the solution. Often the engineers devised expensive technical solutions that satisfied their sense of inventiveness when simpler ideas would have done just as well. The frustration of having their ideas ignored badly affected the morale of the people on the shopfloor. Motivation was low as a consequence.

Now, by contrast, they are almost pampered by management, which goes out of its way to ensure that they get everything they require to sustain the high levels of productivity. On one occasion, for example, the shopfloor workers decided they could do their jobs more effectively if they had a foot-stool to rest on while they were doing assembly work. In the old days they would probably have been told to make do with an old box. But management, now sensitive to their every need, sent for a joiner who came in and made a tailor-made foot stool for each of the women. They each had different requirements according to their physical dimensions. A standard stool for everyone was out of the question. Flexibility of response to varying customer orders is matched by flexibility of response to employees' needs.

As far as Page is concerned, all the pampering is totally justified. He is fully prepared to bow to their needs if it means he can be released from spending all his time dealing with production scheduling problems. While he was organising the installation of one of the new product cells, he was astonished to find that he was only interrupted twice to deal with shopfloor problems. The shopfloor workers were so in control of their own affairs that there was no need to trouble him most of the time. 'It was virtually the first time I was able to get on with something without annoying interruptions. They are running the production work. There's no two ways about it,' he maintains.

RELISH

Page contends that the shopfloor workers have caught on fast about his new role as a coach and a facilitator – and of course they relish their own ability to be in control of their own affairs:

> A lot of people under-estimate how bright the people on the shopfloor are. They think they've got no brains. We've got some very bright people out there. You've got one or two who rely on you a bit more – an arm around the shoulder, a slap on the back, a bit of support, that kind of thing. But you've got some others who don't need you.

Having worked for Black and Decker for 21 years, Page has seen a lot of changes and the empowered management system he now operates is in stark contrast to how things were in the early days when there were five levels of command between management and the shopfloor operator. Then, nobody.dared bypass the level above them. 'You had to go through your immediate chain of command. The people on the shopfloor can speak to anybody now. If they're not happy with me they can go to the next level up.'

The possibility that Page might be making his own job obsolete by taking the empowered route does not appear to trouble him. 'I've got a different role now. It's very satisfying to see this working. I'm quite proud of it – not that it's just down to me.'

WHERE DOES THAT LEAVE THE MANAGER?

Not all managers are as sanguine as Page about what their future role will be when empowered teams take over many of their traditional roles. Notes Tom Standing, head of organisational development for BP Exploration:

> One of the crucial changes necessary to support empowerment is the change in the role of the manager and it is still one of the biggest barriers. What's my job if they're actually doing their own scheduling, deciding on their own organisation and getting their own priorities straight? What's left for me to do? If that's what I used to do, what do I do now?

In BPEX's case the answer tends to be 'you are there to keep enhancing their skills, to keep moving them forward in terms of improvement, to support their learning and their skill development,' says Standing. 'That means you have to be pretty adept at understanding the individual capabilities of people, what their own desires are as far as development is concerned and what could create more productivity and more profitability within the site you're working on.'

Enabling people to develop by understanding their needs, their potential and their progress so far is a major part of the coach's role. The other major part is to remain focused on the bigger picture and to use that to enable employees to motivate and extend themselves. In the sporting analogy of coach one part of the role is the technical and emotional one of helping sports people to believe in and develop themselves; the other is to make them aware of what others are doing, to enter appropriate competitions, to develop new targets with them.

HELPLINE

The question of what will be left for managers to do if empowerment and self-managed work groups are developed to their ultimate effectiveness is something that is exercising the minds of a lot of executives. It is a problem that worries the front-line troops far less.

When the women who operate the Helpline at Digital Equipment in Reading were given the task to design a system that made dealing with customers' telephone enquiries more efficient, they came up with a plan that virtually made management obsolete.

Says Marie-Clare Lounton, one of those entrusted with devising a better system, 'We didn't set out to exclude management. It just happened that way. They simply didn't figure in the new system we came up with.'

In each of the five years Lounton has worked for Digital, management had tried to come up with a better way of organising the Helpline, but each time they gave up and finally handed it over to the people closest to the problem – the call operators themselves. A group of them went off one weekend and debated the gremlins in the system. They drew a flow chart on huge sheets of brown sugar paper itemising the stages a call goes through up to the stage when it is taken up by the department responsible for carrying out the servicing and repairs. Under each stage they listed the problems they encountered and over a series of meetings thrashed out ways to improve the situation.

The main problem was that the system had been devised by a management that was several layers removed from the front line operation. Management had issued instructions about how calls should be answered, but often these instructions did not represent the best way of dealing with a customer's inquiry. The call operators knew from experience how best to keep customers happy, but they often had to go through tiresome routines that did nothing to expedite the solving of the customer's problem.

There were also problems with the technical facilities they worked with. The call operators are divided into separate groups to deal with priority customers and each group operated a different computer system. When they wanted to stand in for each other they found their equipment was not compatible. They even had problems with their headsets which were not efficient or comfortable.

The call operators came up with suggestions to overcome all these problems and when management saw how sensible these were the go-ahead was given to implement their plan. The final plan was worked out at a two-day session at which eight representives of the Helpline came together to share their views. They discussed what would be an ideal working system and compared that with the reality of the situation. 'It was half futuristic and half reality and the two met in the middle,' explains Rhoda Walsh, one of those at the meeting.

Lounton believes they won over the trust and confidence of management by the scientific way they went about the exercise. It included a comprehensive survey of what customers looked for in a Helpline service. 'We asked thousands of people and got all the information together. We know management likes statistics, so we got the statistics together! We had the proof of what the customer wanted. That's the crux of how we are going to work now – for the customer's benefit, not for management.'

Now that the Helpline operators have proved they are the best people to produce a system most likely to keep the customers happy, management at Digital is likely to take even more of a back seat. Lounton says she has only had one face to face meeting with her immediate manager in a six month period and that was not directly to do with work. She wanted to make an inquiry about maternity leave.

Digital management has discovered that the expertise is where it has always been – among the operators themselves. Lounton points out that she learned all she knows about her job from another operator who is a colleague and she in turn had acquired her work knowledge from another colleague.

OUT OF THE PICTURE

Such autonomous work units indeed raise the issue of management's role, but the experience of Chris Lever, a human resources consultant at Digital Equipment Co. Ltd UK, indicates that when management steps right out of the picture there can be serious problems. His anecdote holds out hope for all those managers wondering whether they have any future in the new empowered organisation.

In a previous job with Digital, Lever was part of a group responsible for skills and management development within Digital's UK operations. The manager running the group left the company unexpectedly to take a more senior post in another organisation. Since Digital was unable to replace her immediately the group was virtually turned into a self-managed work group and took over the executive role. 'That was quite a significant time for me,' recalls Lever, 'because I think it was the first time that I had been exposed to the political activity within an organisation. I had always been sheltered from that – the horse trading and all that kind of thing.'

The timing of this radical switch in the way the group was run was not at all propitious as it had just started to ask some searching questions about the suitability of the training programmes it was running and the kind of competencies that were needed to equip Digital management with the skills required to compete in a very aggressive market place. This was hardly the most appropriate time to plunge the group members into a completely new operating style. Recalls Lever:

> 'My recollections of those days is that the team became very powerful very quickly in both a very constructive sense and in a negative way. The group got carried away with the power and we made some very arrogant decisions and some very naive decisions. We rushed in too quickly; we weren't pragmatic. Today I am a lot wiser, but I went along with the decisions then for the sake of consensus.

The group lacked a coach and a facilitator and there was 'nobody working on the external boundaries. The issue with that group was that there weren't sufficient boundaries around, which a manager would have been able to provide. We thought we could do anything and we started to try and do anything, but the reality is you operate within cost structures and within the constraints of the business.'

INSTITUTIONALISED

The group had run over many years what was generally regarded as a successful management development programme which put Digital in the forefront of that kind of work. But the programme had become 'institutionalised' and the company had lost sight of why the programme had been formulated in the first place. As Digital began to find itself in an increasingly competitive market place, the group thought it was time to re-examine whether the training it was providing was appropriate for the new situation the company found itself in.

It went back to base and started asking a number of fundamental questions: What are we in business for? What kind of managers do we need? What skills do we need from the organisation? The answers to those questions, as Lever recalls, were somewhat startling:

> We were shocked to find that the training we provided was actually 180 degrees out of line in some areas. Naively – and acting with some arrogance – we decided to shut down probably between seventy and eighty per cent of all training activity in the organisation. We wanted to understand what the work was so that we could implement a new training

and development programme based on the real needs of the business. We asked exactly the right question. Where we got it wrong was to close up shop – at least that was the perception of our customers. It wasn't totally true because we did carry on with some training.

The precipitous decision to take such drastic action caused, as might have been expected, a wave of consternation among all the people in Digital who had been used to using the well-established training and development programmes. The message that spread throughout the organisation was that power had gone to the heads of the self-managed training group and there needed to be some controls applied to prevent it from running riot.

TASTE OF FREEDOM

When several months later a new manager was appointed to run the group, he faced a no-win situation. It was clear that self-management was not working as it should, but on the other hand the members of the group had tasted the freedom to act autonomously and clearly relished the power that had been theirs to grasp. The new manager was confronted with the problem of having to harness the initiative of the group and yet not kill its enthusiasm for tackling some very real problems at a critical stage in the company's history.

Recalls Lever:

It was a very rough road because there absolutely needed to be some controls and some constraints and some boundaries. Also, we were a group who had tasted what it was to actually make decisions. I think the manager coming in felt that whatever he did was going to be wrong because by this time the group were so up-tight that anyone coming in from outside faced an almost impossible task. In fact, he coped magnificently well, but he was under enormous stress and had to fight every inch of the way.

The final outcome of this cautionary tale was that the manager moved to another company and the training group was absorbed into a different part of the organisation. Several of the group members also left the company, having felt very uncomfortable about the way the group had been run as a self-managed operation.

Looking back on the experience, Lever feels he learned some useful lessons, which probably stood him in good stead in later work he carried out for Digital, particularly in helping to set up self-managed teams in other parts of the organisation:

> I didn't agree with the decision to stop training because I am a fairly pragmatic person. I agreed with the question, I didn't agree with the way they were doing it. Another member of the group also voiced disagreement and was effectively isolated to the point where he wasn't left with much option but to move out. For me, at the time, I had a mortgage to pay, children to feed. It was an interesting personal dilemma and I learned a lot from the experience. I wouldn't take the same action again.

Lever's subsequent experience with Digital, as a group effectiveness portfolio manager, was far more positive. He was given a high degree of autonomy to run his own budget and develop various products and processes, but he operated under 'a very strong manager, who, as he came to grips with our roles and grew comfortable with them, began to delegate and to move out of the day-to-day operations much more. Then he started to perform what I see as the critical role of working back into the organisation.

> My memory is of increasing authority, increasing empowerment to the extent where virtually I had very little lead on a day-to-day basis from management. I organised my own time. I was very clear about my goals and I was very clear about what I was going to get measured on. How I achieved it was absolutely down to me. Of all my time in Digital, I think that was the most significant in helping me understand what I am capable of and almost what my inner resources and inner capabilities are.

Lever helped to set up the high performance administration teams in Digital's northern region outlined in the previous chapter on empowerment and again he discovered that the role of the manager can be critical to success. He was involved in examining how well the work teams operated and their relationship to management. He recalls that:

> one of the things we struggled with was specifically the role of the manager, because when we were implementing what was quite a complex initiative, a lot of attention had been paid to training the teams in new

systems and new ways of working, but very little attention had been paid originally to the role of the manager. The consequence was that the teams were getting very large messages about being empowered, being more skilled in many different areas, but the managers were managing that newness in exactly the same way as they always had. Little attention had originally been given to the role of the manager and the applicability of the style. People were just managing in the old way and there was a lot of tension. That's not a criticism of the managers. That's how it was.

REBELLION

Often managers recognise the need for a change of style, but are simply unable to make the necessary adjustment. Paul DeSouza, a regional property manager at Digital, was very unhappy when the manager in charge of his department announced that he and the rest of his colleagues were going to be turned into a self-managed work group. They had worked together as a team for a number of years and felt that they already operated as a well-functioning group. They all got on well together at work and spent a lot of time together socially.

DeSouza and his colleagues rebelled against the idea of being forced into a prescribed operating mode dictated by an outside consultant. They believed it would undermine working relationships that had developed naturally and had worked to everyone's satisfaction for a number of years. DeSouza argued that he and his colleagues should be allowed to continue working in the way that best suited them, but their manager insisted that they should become empowered!

What DeSouza did not know at the time was that the senior manager they reported to had planned to take early retirement and that, as he puts it, there was 'a hidden agenda'. She wanted the property team to become more self-reliant so that they would be able to operate as a more autonomous work unit after she had left the company. But De Souza claims she had never made this explicit at the outset and he resented being kept in the dark.

He eventually sat down with the consultant Digital had brought in to help set up self-managed teams in various parts of the organisation and worked out a system of operating that was more in tune with the way they had always worked. According to DeSouza, the consultant had to agree that they were virtually already a self-managed team. 'What they were after is something we couldn't actually get hold of, something that wasn't tangible. We couldn't see what the result would be at the end. What they were after was behaviours. We were getting those at the time because we knew each other inside out.'

'Don't get me wrong,' he adds, 'I believe in SMTs (self-managed teams). I believe in the fact that you have to work as a team moving in one direction. By the sheer nature of our operation we have to; otherwise we would sink. We have been doing that for years, because we all know in which direction we have to head. The SMT element is there.'

UNABLE TO LET GO

To add to the dilemma, DeSouza and his colleagues felt that their manager was not keeping to her side of the bargain. She was not able to stand back and let them run their own affairs. She was not some-body who could keep to the sidelines. She enjoyed the hustle and bustle of negotiating over space requirements, for example, with the Digital units using the property department's services. She had a financial background and was very reluctant, in DeSouza's opinion, to let go the purse strings of budgetary control.

Maintains DeSouza:

> The manager was not prepared to release the empowerment. We said: 'If you are saying to us we are a self-managed team, then as far as we're concerned, technically speaking, you should be able to sit on the side-lines and watch us manage'. Her response was: 'Well, no, you can't; I've got to direct you.' We said: 'Hang on, we're not an SMT if we haven't got any empowerment'.

A DIFFERENT KETTLE OF FISH

DeSouza and his colleagues are much happier with the manager they operate under today:

> He's a different kettle of fish – a stand-off individual, very clever from an academic point of view. I don't have a problem with that. I think it's excellent because he sees things from a different perspective. What he's basically saying to us is: 'You're the professionals; get on with it'. We are saying: 'Great, let us get on with it. We'll guide you and you can go and do the presentations.' We've got that at last and we haven't looked back.

DeSouza sees a stark contrast with the present working climate and how it used to be under the former manager:

> She was a coach and good supporter, but she dabbled and interfered all the time and in many respects tried to do our jobs for us. She would go and negotiate all the various space elements for our business with the customers. She literally commanded the whole of the budget, which was something like £46 million, and trimmed and cut it whenever she wanted without consulting us. There was no strategy. It was firefighting. There was no plan because we couldn't get together with her to get a business plan.

By contrast, DeSouza's current manager concentrates on planning and strategy. 'He is a strategist, a planner and a processor. He says: "you are the experts, you get on with the job. If you need support or direction, I'm here for you; otherwise don't cause me too many problems because you have the power and the authority to drive the business for us".'

He also lobbies the Digital board of management on the property department's behalf to 'get decisions, direction and strategic intent – i.e. a business plan, because if you're not careful property will drive the business rather than the other way round. In fact it has happened,' says DeSouza.

MAINTAINING MOMENTUM

One of the key roles of a manager in today's empowered environment is to sustain the momentum. If managers are only half-hearted about empowered teams or simply pay lip service to the idea, the thrust of the programme will soon wane and will be in danger of fizzling out.

Black and Decker introduced empowered teams to its accessories plant at Spennymoor in County Durham, some four years ago. Everybody from the general manager to the janitor took part in off-site sessions to learn more about what constitutes effective teamworking. Everybody returned to work highly enthusiastic about the idea and convinced it was the right direction to go in.

Recalls Trevor Deighton, technical support manager of the European accessories division, 'Instead of having supervisors, people hitting the numbers and no sense of pride and ownership, we went to a team structure. We appointed the team leaders we have today. Those team leaders report directly to the business team manager, reducing the hierarchy from four to three layers.'

Recognising the key role team leaders would play, Black and Decker decided to select them using psychometric testing, a technique normally reserved for applicants for management posts. Using it for this level of job was quite revolutionary for Black and Decker.

Four years later, the company is not convinced it selected people of a sufficient calibre to carry the onerous task of making teamwork a success. Says Deighton, 'I don't know if we didn't give them the right level of training or whether, in all honesty, we didn't pitch the team leader job at a high enough calibre of person, because the team leader role is a key role. He's a coach, a trainer and a facilitator. That's asking an awful lot of anybody. One of the common mistakes – and we've fallen into it – is not getting the right calibre of people.'

To facilitate teamworking, the accessories plant at Spennymoor switched from a process-based environment to a cell structure of eight product-based teams. It allowed teams to be formed around a single product, ranging from screwdrivers to jigsaws, which they make in their entirety. Says Deighton, 'I don't know what's more important, the structure or the teamworking, but both of them side by side are very powerful.'

The switch to empowered teams also introduced much greater flexibility into the operation. 'We used to have a low number of batches, high run. We went to a high number of batches, low run,' elaborates Deighton. 'Job sizes went from 5,000 to 500.'

There was a huge amount of enthusiasm for the new way of working, but what Black and Decker had underestimated was the resistance they were likely to encounter from old-guard managers who were entrenched in the old ways of striving to meet production targets through a control and command style that they had practised over many years. Says Deighton, 'We found it incredibly difficult to sustain the momentum. It's the balance between improving and maintaining. It's very easy to fall back on the controlled world of hitting the numbers. Your first job is to hit the numbers, not to improve the numbers for tomorrow.'

Deighton sees two discrete elements to a business:

> You've got to hit the numbers, but you also need to provide the structure that will move the business on. If you think it is all going to happen by these people who are managing today's numbers, you're kidding yourself. The resistance is not overt. A lot of people are too long in the tooth to know that you cannot overtly reject these things, but there are ways and means.

FRUITS OF SUCCESS

Empowerment enthusiasts would argue that as the teams taste the fruits of their successes, the continuous improvement would come of its own accord. Success breeds success. But Deighton believes it depends on the support empowered teams receive from management. 'One of the problems is how people are managed and people easily step back into the old ways and that's indeed what happened here. Some of the traditional managers thought this was just another management fad.'

Deighton is determined to resist that view. 'It's a management fad that isn't going away. Black and Decker has followed up with a total quality programme and we have core values – integrity, excellence, teamwork and innovation. The teamwork, total quality ethos is here to stay. It's not a six months exercise.'

Where empowerment is taking hold strongly in Black and Decker you tend to find a manager who believes in it wholeheartedly and drives it forward with determination – someone like Francis Barnish, operations manager of the Minicraft business. Deighton wonders if teamworking at Minicraft would continue to prosper if Barnish moved elsewhere. 'The overriding feeling is that managers supporting this have to be dedicated, focused, fanatical about the benefits you can get out of it.'

THE IDEAL MANAGER?

Managers at Black and Decker recently sat down together and tried to draw up a model of what they thought a good manager ought to be. They then measured themselves against it. They each sent the results to ten colleagues, three senior executives, four peers and three subordinates, who added their views anonymously. It is using the conclusions as the basis of a management development programme.

Deighton recognises that he too will have to adapt his management style to take account of the new empowered environment. 'On my psychometrics I've always come out very strong on leadership – like the captain of a football team. I've had to refine that. I've become conscious of my strengths and shortcomings and tried to adapt.'

Deighton grew up in the old autocratic manufacturing environment, but by the time he was made a manager that had already become discredited. 'I saw the downside of it, so hopefully I've modified my behaviour accordingly.'

However, when he worked as a manufacturing superintendent he was shocked to be told by one of his more outspoken staff members that 'everyone was terrified of me'. The fact that he is 6 ft 6 in tall may have had something to do with it, but it brought Deighton up sharp. 'It made me stop and think because I really didn't view myself like that at all.'

The irony is that change for the better that evolves over a period of time is often not fully appreciated.

> Sometimes people forget where we've come from. I don't know how much belief there is on the shopfloor, for want of a better term. With some of my guys it's as if we have done nothing. I just take them back two or three years to the old days when our only objective was labour efficiency, not customer satisfaction or service levels. We used to make

the wrong product and build excessive inventory and we weren't building what the customer wanted, but our labour efficiency was high. Measures are important but I think some organisations need to change some of their measures.

PEOPLE MANAGEMENT

In many cases companies set on the empowerment route may feel that they are fighting a losing battle in trying to bring about the necessary radical changes of management style. They feel their chances of success are greatly enhanced if they concentrate on the recruitment stage. Job advertisements even for highly technical management posts are now stressing the man-management elements of the work rather than dwelling on technological know-how. A lot of companies argue that it is much easier to train people in technical skills than it is to change behaviour.

At Nuclear Electric, where managerial job descriptions used to be eighty per cent technical and twenty per cent skills in people-handling, they have now virtually reversed the ratio, so vital are coaching and facilitating skills in the group's more empowered management approach.

BP is taking a similar view. Says Tom Standing, BP Exploration's head of organisational development:

> What we are after in BPEX is getting a better balance between task and people skills. We knew we had a lot of very good task managers and technicians, but we felt they had very little skill in working with people. They were good geologists, good petroleum engineers, good drillers, so they were put into important management jobs, but a lot of them were fairly blind to the people side of things.

To emphasise its need for a different kind of manager, BPEX conducts an upward feedback process annually, in which staff at all levels are asked to evaluate their managers according to over twenty criteria. The resulting report serves as a discussion point between the manager and his team. With the aid of a facilitator they debate whether there could be any improvements in the manager's style in relationship to the empowered environment. Says Standing:

The process has been very useful in keeping the issues right out there in front for every team leader in the organisation right up to John Browne (BPEX's chief executive), who does an upward feedback every year too. That's a very powerful demonstration to staff that we are serious about shifting the power balance. The results have been very supportive of the idea that managers are taking seriously this empowerment idea.

EXPERTISE AND EXPERIENCE

In the traditional command and control organisation, the function of the manager has been to pass orders down the line and make sure they were carried out. Managerial expertise was seen to be a function of experience. By the time they reached the top managers had accumulated a lot of experience and they decided what to do based on that experience. Senior managers, through their over-view, gain more experience than others although it may be limited to only one or two functions. Seniority and experience made managers adept at deciding what has to be done and checking that it is carried out. They passed instructions down the line to those who were less experienced.

It is assumed that managers are developed, but a lot of the development is simply by experience. Such experience may confirm the value of doing things in a particular way or it may provide the basis for seeing things in an entirely different way, although that seems less usual. The amount of learning which takes place depends on the managers' skill in developing from their experience. The more narrow that experience the less the stimulus to learn.

Qualifying for promotion in the organisational pyramid is usually a matter of performing well in the current job. Performing well in the current job is not just a matter of results, it is a matter of conforming to expectations – from above and below. Such conformance includes fulfilling the traditional managerial role.

That traditional role, as conceived in a command and control structured organisation, dealt with management as planning, organising, directing and controlling. It involved identifying the needed activities, acquiring the appropriate resources, organising them most efficiently, allocating tasks, specifying performance standards, monitoring and correcting performance. It was a simple hierarchic tell process.

Perhaps the most fascinating aspect of this conception of management is that so many managers found it so difficult to do. The numbers of managers on time management programmes bear ample testimony to the difficulties of identifying organisational and personal priorities. Current interest in Just in Time (JIT) manufacturing systems, in lean production systems, in total quality management and in process re-engineering reflect the difficulties that managers have in planning, organising, directing and controlling.

For the most part those difficulties are not a simple function of personal inadequacy or lack of development, although these may compound the problem. Rather, they reflect the increasing complexity of trying to manage in a rapidly changing world using techniques and conceptual frameworks developed in a less turbulent, less chaotic environment. Repeated conversations with managers reveal their frustration at their lack of time to plan, at the interruptions which prevent them getting on with their 'work', their difficulty in organising complex resources, their inability to motivate and enthuse their staff and their reluctance to confront and resolve sub-standard performance.

RECIPE FOR FRUSTRATION

Trying to manage in a changing world with outdated concepts is a potent recipe for frustration and disappointment. Many managers still harp back to the planning, organising, directing and control model and they feel guilty when they don't work that way. The relief evident in many managers as they talked about their experience of empowerment and the change in their role was the relief of those for whom concepts had caught up with the demands placed upon them and with their values.

Some of this is not new. In the 1970s Henry Mintzberg, the Canadian management guru, attempted to reconcile theory and reality by describing what managers actually did. He found that they performed an enormous variety of very quick tasks. In some of his studies they spent as little as twenty seconds on a particular transaction. Even in the case of a chief executive, the average transaction only took nine minutes, and that included some two or three hour board meetings, so other transactions by definition were much shorter. Managerial work, in this account, was a continuing series of interruptions.

Mintzberg identified three major role sets that managers occupied. These were interpersonal, informational and decisional. The emphasis implied in the former two reflects the extent to which management had shifted. Managers emerge as boundary managers – inside and outside the organisation, as spreaders of information laterally and vertically, and as strategists determining new initiatives and bargaining for resources to seize the opportunities. The manager in an empowered organisation appears as a more fully developed version of that model.

REVOLUTION

A typical manager who has trouble controlling his time, locks himself away in his office trying to wade through numerous reports, never stopping to ask why he is doing it. To cope with all these reports, he shuts his door to try to keep people from interrupting him. He constructs elaborate defences of secretaries, appointments and written communications. But still, with the insistence of the man from Porlock, they keep knocking at his door. The reality is that his job as a manager is actually dealing with people and the rest of it is of little importance by comparison. Yet many managers, even if they accept that intellectually, still have real difficulty believing it in their hearts.

Many managers will say, 'It's all very well talking about developing people, but I don't have time for that. I've got work to do.' If you ask these same managers whether they believe they would be better or worse off with a developed work force, they readily admit they would be better off. Worse are those managers who complain about the quality of their staff and the need to do everything themselves but still cannot see an alternative. Managers know that their job is fire prevention or household security or some other strategic objective but continue to encumber themselves with sand buckets, hose pipes and extinguishers as they continue their customary firefighting.

The issue here is a revolution in the way managers think about their jobs. The impact of that cannot be underestimated. Managers are discovering that their job is no longer about being more experienced than their staff. It is no longer about being more knowledgeable or more certain than their staff. All that is not easy to accept, particularly if the manager still secretly believes his role is to plan, organise, direct and control. How can he change unless the staff respect and value him? But in changing he would diminish their current grounds for respecting and valuing him.

It can be disconcerting to say the least to be in charge of something you don't know much about. It can be even more frightening if the planning, organising, directing and controlling is handed over to the empowered work team itself. If the team is going to take responsibility for planning and organising their own work; if they're going to become their own motivators and monitors; if they're going to allocate the work among themselves, what role is there left for the first-line supervisor or manager? That's quite a mind-boggling concept to absorb. It doesn't help either that all this is happening during the severest recession since the 1930s and when companies are delayering their organisations to become more efficient with the inevitable result that thousands of managers – particularly middle managers – are finding themselves made redundant.

At a time when organisations are downsizing, managers are being asked to co-operate in a process which says 'We know what you're supposed to do, but the people who work for you are going to do it instead'. It would be surprising if that did not make a lot of managers feel very uneasy and insecure.

It is perhaps understandable, therefore, that even those managers who are persuaded intellectually about the merits of empowerment find themselves puting up real emotional resistance to the whole idea.

EXPECTATIONS

There are also problems about expectations. If managers in the past have always operated on the plan, organise, direct and control model, the expectations of their subordinates are that they will continue to operate in that mode. What expectations, on the whole, do subordinates have of themselves? Not very much. They are accustomed to obeying instructions without giving much thought to whether they are performing as effectively as they might be. If the instructions don't work, it is not the employee's fault because he isn't in charge of the process. The old system creates sets of expectations from the work force who don't think they have a responsibility to contribute. They don't feel they need to be aware of what they are doing or take responsibility for it.

This reinforces the manager's own preconceptions that the subordinates are neither capable nor willing to take on more responsibility. At the same time it creates the situation where the manager has to be aware of everything and take charge of everything although this is humanly impossible and totally undesirable. That is not a situation that is manageable.

The organisation itself will convey expectations. Through the behaviour of more senior managers who may continue to operate in the old style, perhaps because they are further from the front-line. Through appraisal and reward systems which have moved towards accentuating individual responsibility. Through performance-related pay systems which reinforce the message that performance is down to the manager. Through promotion patterns which provide powerful signals about what kinds of behaviour are regarded most favourably further up the organisation. Such behaviour may be the opposite of that desired by subordinates, but there are few organisations where subordinates determine promotions.

There is for many a real threat and fear attached to the notion of the manager as coach. It is not simply a question of helping managers to understand how they can do it. It is also about offering assurances, because managers may think that they were pretty good at the old plan, organise, direct and control approach. Indeed, they may well have been good at it. At least coaching provides an alternative positive role, provided managers can master the change of style outlined in the next three chapters. In many cases, that means casting off habits of a working lifetime. Nobody is under any illusion that it is an easy switch to make.

LEADERS NOT SUPERVISORS

Colin Toogood runs the Royal Mail's sorting office at Plymouth, where a new system of self-checking is fundamentally changing the relationship between first-line managers and the sorting staff. Toogood believes that devolving greater responsibility to front-line staff enables managers to become leaders rather than supervisors of routine work:

> A leader needs clearly to set the goals and outline the tasks that are required. Then he needs to allocate responsibilities. He needs to measure how things are progressing in those work areas against the goals that were set and support the team in achieving them. Basically, it's a question of identifying the task and who is going to do it and then supporting the process.

Toogood considers it a primary role of management to help staff acquire the new skills necessary for them to tackle the higher level responsibilities. These could be presentational skills or some sort of financial awareness or training in cost control.

> In the past budgets were not deemed to be the responsibility of supervisors, for example. That was always done by the finance manager even though ninety-nine per cent of it was spent operationally. The team leader is the one who is going to have to gain the knowledge of what it is actually costing him to run his work area. What's needed is the information technology support and financial skills training.

Perhaps the most crucial difference between leadership and supervision is that supervision emphasises monitoring and control, leadership direction and motivation. In the Royal Mail the shift away from supervision is a shift towards self-monitoring and self-control. In other organisations where there is more scope to determine the task the move might be towards determining direction.

ROLE MODEL

Rank Xerox, too, believes that empowerment is requiring managers to take on more of a leadership role. It has developed a programme with Ashridge Management College to achieve just that. Some 100 managers from its European headquarters in Marlow, Bucks., and from its UK operating companies have so far been through the course. Observes Clare Harding, quality consultant at Marlow:

> A lot of time is being spent looking at the role of the manager changing to that of leader. Coaching is one element of that, but just as important as coaching people in various aspects of their task, he's got to be a role model himself. The leader has got to be the strategic thinker; he's got to be the facilitator; he's also got to be the barrier buster to help his team perform as effectively as they can. So there has to be a whole series of skills and attributes that the manager is going to have to take on board. Coaching is certainly one of those.
>
> I think you do need somebody the team can focus on to help them with interface issues, who can head them in the right direction if they come up against barriers outside their own province or control, but which need to be addressed. That leader can and should help remove those barriers for them to help get them entry, say, into different parts of the organisation.

That is a view that is endorsed by Ralph Orrico, executive director of group resources at Marlow:

> Current managers, wherever they are in the organisation, need to be trained in terms of moving them from this command and control role to much more of a leadership kind of role. Every company has a lot of people who are very good at managing; what we're really trying to do is enlarge that. You're still going to have to control certain things. You need a manager who can be a coach or counsellor, but you also need someone to control things, so the whole leadership aspect needs to be changed with a lot of our managers in helping them to make their people and their organisations more productive.

Orrico warns that the new approach will not immediately make everyone's lives a lot easier. Quite the contrary. 'It's not made my life easier,' he admits. 'It's probably not made the staff's life any easier because they now have to reach into some things they didn't have to do in the past.'

He also notes that it is hard for employees to accept that they are no longer constrained by the old hierarchical structure and pecking order. The less experienced employees who were in a more subordinate role in the previous structure find it hard to break free of former habits and assert themselves in the new empowered environment. Says Orrico:

> In the early days I would see the same people I always saw. They were always on my calendar; they were always on my door step. Little by little I'm beginning to see all the people beginning to come in and ask for an hour of my time or review with me something they have done. They are participating more at staff meetings. It takes time on both sides. It takes time for the manager to adjust to these different levels that are now all on the same plain.
>
> It also takes time for the individuals themselves to feel comfortable in this new flat organisation. There's a lot of comfort in having a couple of layers ahead of you, because if things go wrong there's always somebody up the line that will catch it.

NO LONGER THE BOSS

Bryan Jackson, director of human resources and corporate affairs at Toyota UK, observes that the manager in the empowered organisation may well cease to be the boss in the old sense, but his support or coaching role still means that he must provide 'direction, knowledge and resources to his staff. And within this framework he needs to ensure that there are personal development and team goals and these must, of course, be measurable. This doesn't mean retreating behind a desk or into an office on the fifth floor.'

Jackson confirms that it is not easy for British managers to adapt to the empowered approach that has become a way of life in Japanese companies:

> A Japanese manager will monitor and tutor one of his team, yet hold back and watch that person make a mistake. Then the manager will explain how the mistake came about and help the person avoid that mistake again.
>
> A manager new to empowerment will see the mistake coming and wade

in. The problem may be avoided but the lesson may not be fully appreciated by the student. And then, if the mistake is repeated both parties are upset: the student feels inadequate and the manager frustrated. In actual fact, taking an empowered view, it should be the student who feels frustrated and the manager inadequate.

Jackson has a very clear view of the difference between the old command and control approach and the new style 'empowering' managers:

> Old style managers like to think of themselves as the boss. After all, they're used to taking responsibilities; this means they're used to taking decisions alone. If you can do that, what's the point of sharing information?
>
> New style managers understand their role as coach and share information and invite others to contribute to the decision making to share ownership of the ultimate decision.
>
> The difference is easy to spot if you compare the efforts of a team with a new style manager or coach to a team with the old style manager. Set a task for both teams. The old style authoritarian manager will decide how it will be done, by whom and when. If it's a new task the team may fail because they lack commitment. If they succeed there is no shared feeling of achievement because they simply did what they were told.
>
> The new manager will present the task to the team and ask for their suggestions. As coach, he or she will help the team evaluate their suggestions, sort out priorities and gain consensus on how to proceed. The team will be committed to the success of the project and will each share in the achievement. Should it fail, there will be no apportionment of individual blame. They all recognise there was something wrong with *their* system and look for ways of making improvements.

HOW EMPLOYEES PERCEIVE THE CHANGED ROLE OF THE MANAGER

A lot of managers may feel their efforts to change their operating style go unnoticed, but Ian Garbutt, energy efficiency officer at Nuclear Electric's Hartlepool station, is lavish in his praise for the way his manager has given him his head since he was made a team leader. He has been put in charge of a team of five volunteers to spearhead a drive to save energy as part of a general cost-cutting campaign. Garbutt reports to the station's production manager, who has empowered him to tackle the task in the way he best sees fit.

Garbutt, who recalls the hierarchical structure of the old GECB with a shudder, is wildly enthusiastic about the degree of autonomy he has been given:

> You're responsible for your own finances, your own staffing, your own resources. I have my own budget for the energy efficiency group. That's something a second engineer wouldn't have had in a hundred years under the old hierarchical structure. The ownership of the job has made me highly motivated.

Garbutt now sees the manager he reports to very much as a hands-off coach. 'He says it's your group, your money, your staff and your resources. Obviously, if he asks for justification I have to give it, but that's all. I inform him regularly what is happening within the team and any schemes we're looking at. He isn't hovering over me all the time.'

Being allowed to run his own affairs has transformed Garbutt's life and his attitude to work. 'I'm amazed at the change in myself. Six months ago I wasn't highly motivated. I arrived at the station, I worked and I went home. I would happily work here fifteen hours a day now.'

A few months prior to being given the increased responsibility Garbutt was so disenchanted with life at Nuclear Electric he had started looking for another job. Now leaving the Hartlepool station is the last thing on his mind. 'The views I had of Nuclear Electric, this station, everything really, has absolutely altered. The motivating factor is the recognition and the fact I have increased status and responsibility.'

4

COACHING IN SPORT AND BUSINESS

Gerry Callanan is one of a team of project managers at Sainsbury's working on the installation of a new sales-based ordering system (SABRE) into the retail group's stores throughout the country. As one of the projects he undertook as part of an MBA programme the UK retail group runs in conjunction with City University Business School, he decided to explore the idea of developing coaching techniques. A one-time football coach, Callanan is particularly interested in the links between sports coaching and business.

As part of the research he went to watch Watford Football Club practising for an important match to see first-hand the coaching style they used. Recalls Callanan:

> I had read articles about the manager as coach and I wanted to explore the parallels with sport. I didn't see much coaching going on at Watford. It was more instructional – 'Run around that cone! Beat the man! Have a shot at target!' – that sort of thing. It was more like drill really.

But when Callanan heard about a coaching programme which combined sport and learning he decided to try it out. He was so impressed with what he learned that he sought permission from Sainsbury's senior management to organise a prototype programme for some of his colleagues on the SABRE project.

He saw coaching as the ideal way to persuade the branches to use the new computerised ordering system to optimum effect. Points out Callanan, 'There is a difference between getting a system installed and making sure that it gets used and that the stores own it and take responsibility for it.'

With the backing of his senior manager, Callanan arranged a two-day pilot course on coaching and team building for twelve members of the SABRE project group.

EVERY DAY IS A PERFORMANCE

Judith Evans, Sainsbury's director of corporate personnel, believes that the sports coach analogy is particularly appropriate to a large-scale retail operation. 'Well over fifty per cent of our staff meet the customer on a regular basis. So they are performing. The store every day is a performance.'

Taking the idea that staff 'perform' with internal or external customers allows the introduction of coaching ideas from sport and entertainment. In both industries coaches may be seen to divide between those who drill trainees to perform in a particular manner chosen by the coach and those coaches who see their responsibility as developing the innate talent and potential of the trainee while readily acknowledging that talent may be greater than the coach's.

Callanan was able to identify clear changes in his behaviour as a result of studying the links between sports coaching and business management. 'It's rather subjective, but I do feel the way I deal with people has changed as a result of this project – not just the training course, but as a result of gathering information about the whole issue. I think I am more aware of coaching opportunities. Don't get me wrong. I still let opportunities pass me by. Occasionally, I'll still be directive. But I think I catch more of the opportunities than I previously did.'

The project of installing the new sales-based order system into Sainsbury's stores is providing an excellent opportunity for Callanan and his team to test out their mastery of coaching techniques. 'One of the key result areas is the extent to which the stores want to use the system and whether they continue to use it effectively after we have gone out the door,' he notes. 'You can always make a system tick over. To maximise the benefits you must want to use it.'

It might be expected that the staff running the stores would embrace wholeheartedly a system that is likely to increase their efficiency and obviate the need for manual operations. But people tend to be a lot more content with the systems they have grown up with and which they have been operating perfectly happily for some time. There is always an element of 'better the devil you know.'

Says Callanan, 'They love the current ordering system. They've all been inducted into the company with it and all of a sudden we're coming along and saying here is a new system which does all these wonderful things. They need to be persuaded it will actually work for them.'

OWNING THE SYSTEM

Callanan is convinced that coaching is the way to get the stores' staff to own the system.

> The coaching philosophy is the approach we want to use. We aren't going there to instruct people. In the past, we have gone into the branches and sat down with the manager and key people and told them what they were going to get. The big turnaround is that we've geared ourselves up to go in and say: 'you know you've got a sales-based ordering system coming; what benefits do you expect from that? What do you want to get from it?'
>
> With company pilots, although the base software does certain things, you can adapt it for operational use. Some managers may check ordering levels three times a day; others just once in the morning. So there is some freedom even with systems development. But the actual ownership of the system is what we are trying to get across.

Coaching, as Callanan defines it, is highly interactive between coach and trainee. Yes, coaches have a level of expertise in the technical area, but their real expertise is in the interaction with the trainees, using questions to highlight their needs and their suggestions and ideas as to how those are best met. Coaching in this mode assumes a fundamental equality of partnership rather than the power gulf of hierarchy built into traditional models of management.

PART OF THE AGENDA

Coaching has long been an integral part of Sainsbury's management development agenda. Says Evans:

> That's because we are a very fast-moving business and one in which it is very helpful to be able to develop people through the work that they're doing on the job as opposed to having to take them away to a situation which has nothing to do with what they're meant to be doing.
>
> Because it's a hands-on environment, it has always been very attractive to us to work on coaching. It's been featured in our management development programme for many years and more recently we have been looking at ways in which we can use the physical environment to help people to learn coaching.

This long-time association with coaching and its role on the management development agenda undoubtedly made it easier for Callanan to try a new approach with SABRE. It could also be argued that that long-time association predisposed Callanan to look at coaching. The impact of becoming a coach is far less threatening in an environment where such ideas are common currency. Changing circumstances appear to have appreciated the value of coaching against other forms of management.

INSPIRATION

A growing number of commercial organisations are turning to top sportsmen for advice on how to motivate their staff. The view is growing that sporting heroes like Will Carling, captain of the English rugby team, can be as inspirational in the business arena as they are on the playing field.

The idea is particularly appealing to organisations in the forefront of the empowerment movement which aims to maximise the potential of front-line employees and free up senior management to tackle urgent strategic issues. It is widely believed that this requires executives to switch from the traditional command and control mode of management to a coaching style. It is also appealing to those who recognise that comand and control systems failed to engage fully employees' commitment to, or belief in, the organisation's aspirations. Growing competitive pressures have raised the stakes and the rewards. Organisations cannot afford the luxury of unrecognised or un-utilised talents while job insecurity encourages employees to search for opportunities to develop themselves.

Brian Baldock, deputy chairman of Guinness plc and chairman of the Lord's Taverners, sees very strong links between sport and business. Writing in the July 1993 issue of *Management Today*, he declared:

> Sport is not just about the excitement of the game or the race. It is about the bridge which it builds between people of all types, cultures and interests. It is about the sharing and single-minded pursuit of common goals, about striving to achieve outstanding performance, about teamwork, communication, leadership and coaching, and ultimately, of course, it is about success.
>
> In sports, individual performance is the key to achievement. I believe that the same could be said to be true of business. Yet the sort of lessons we can learn from the sports field appear all too often to be overlooked in the boardroom. Perhaps it is because the intellectual approach has superseded this somewhat more emotional and pragmatic system.

An obvious analogy is the fact that a sports coach puts a lot of effort into preparing a team for match day, but that once the game is underway he is confined to the sidelines. Only the team members can execute the game plan. Similarly, empowering organisations coach their employees for the task in hand and then leave them to get on with it free from interference. As managers increasingly find themselves supervising staff more expert than they are (i.e. computer programmers), this approach is becoming not simply desirable but a necessity. Sports coaching has made enormous strides which have been largely unrecognised by business. Concentration on technique – analogous to business's concentration on technical knowledge – has been extended by awareness of the mental and emotional demands of top-class performance.

Observes Baldock in *Management Today*:

> Coaching is critical, in my view, because while not everyone can be a

leader, everyone can be a coach. Coaches do not have to be more skilled than the person they are coaching, but they must be able to add value to the person's development – personal or professional – by virtue of developed skills of observation and explanation and, probably most important of all, by practical demonstration.

While many might argue with Baldock's observation that not everyone can be a leader his comments on the importance of observation, explanation and demonstration would find widespread support. Implicit in his comments is the importance of feedback. Everyone can provide feedback, everyone can develop their skills of giving and receiving feedback.

A BETTER GAME OF GOLF

'It's a big challenge for business managers to enable their subordinates to do a better job than they could probably do, but it's absolutely critical in coaching,' says David Whitaker, who coached the English hockey team to a gold medal in the Seoul Olympics in Korea in 1988. He has joined forces with David Hemery, the Olympic hurdler and Sir John Whitmore, the former European racing car champion, to form Performance Consultants. Their clients range from Barclays Bank and Woolwich Building Society to shoemakers Clarks International and Kent County Constabulary.

A video produced in conjunction with Barclays illustrates the philosophy behind the coaching methods devised by Performance Consultants. It shows two novice golfers, one being taught by a professional instructor and the other by John Whitmore, who is not a golf player. Whitmore achieves quicker results by involving his trainee in deciding for herself how best to improve her technique.

'Just by raising awareness you can improve the way you hit a golf ball, no matter what your standard,' insists Whitaker. 'That's mind-blowing to some people because it really hits at some preconceived notions about how to improve people's performance. It's actually saying to the expert that just telling people all you know is perhaps not the best way. If you watch a golf pro when he teaches somebody, he teaches them his own way when in fact we all hit the ball differently. We are all different human beings.'

Similar coaching methods are demonstrated in the video to help three Barclays' employees to tackle various problems ranging from bad time management and poor morale to difficulties in turning sales leads into firm orders.

Ian Wigston, Barclays' director of resource development – markets, became sold on coaching after attending the standard two day course run by Whitaker and his colleagues. He then had to convince 'fairly sceptical' senior management at Barclays that 'somebody with a predominantly sporting background could teach hard-nosed businessmen some new lessons.' Some pilot programmes were then introduced into sales management at Barclays, an area Wigston felt could benefit considerably from the coaching approach.

He sees a clear correlation between the methods used in sports coaching and the need to improve individual performances in business. 'The role of the coach in business,' he observes, 'is not just to tell the performer how to score goals more frequently; it's to raise the awareness of the performer and get him to take responsibility for what he is doing.'

There is strong evidence that the sports coaching approach significantly improved the scoring rate of Barclays' sales managers. The regions used in the pilot programme far exceeded the sales targets they were set. 'We could attribute a big part of that directly back to the work that the coaching team had done,' claims Wigston.

CLASHING CULTURES

Wigston was so convinced he was on the right track that he hired David Whitaker to become his personal coach for a difficult exercise involving the merger of two Barclays' businesses with clashing cultures. The integration had been recommended by a firm of outside consultants, but it had been decided to undertake the implementation phase internally.

> Our task was to implement a very difficult change management agenda and we had to create the infrastructure that ideally would have existed if the firm of consultants had been allowed to implement the programme

their way. The bank had said that we could do it for ourselves and had underestimated the degree of implementation resource required, so I used what I regarded as a very wise and available implementation resource, which was my coach.

The integration was completed while at the same time achieving record profits. 'In other words, we kept our eye on the ball, kept scoring goals whilst putting on the same uniform,' suggests Wigston.

Coaching is now one of the techniques employed at a Barclays' innovation centre (known as a resource development unit) recently set up by Wigston. It makes its services available to outside organisations as well as helping bring an innovative approach to problem solving within the bank.

'We don't generate the ideas so much as enable the people we work with to generate the ideas,' explains Wigston. 'We coach them using different proceses to bring out ideas which are within their minds, but may not have been liberated by the organisation, whether it's Barclays or any other business.'

The biggest problem Wigston has come up against has been:

coaching people to realise that they have the ability to grow themselves. They have to realise it themselves and the only way to achieve that is by trying it out, so we often have to lead people into it. It's a question of giving people a licence to be creative. It's realising that everybody has some form of creativity within them, but the problem frequently is that it is left at home rather than brought to the work place. If the individual doesn't believe that the organisation wants their brainpower, except in a very narrow way, then motivation won't bring it to the table. It needs more than motivation.

The relation between empowerment as a general approach, and coaching as a very powerful means of delivering that approach, is reflected in Wigston's comments. There is more to empowerment than coaching alone can deliver, but coaching is an immensely powerful vehicle enabling managers and staff to adapt to the new way of working.

TELLING STYLE

Whitaker became disenchanted with the traditional telling style of coaching when he played hockey internationally for England. He resented being told what to do by a coach who was technically less proficient than he was.

> I was being told how to play by an ex-international player who hadn't played for ten years, had never played my position and didn't truly understand what was happening on the field. At best, I took what I heard from the coaches, fitted it with what I knew truly happened on the field and found a synthesis. At worst, I listened to what they said, realised it didn't fit with what the reality was and did my own thing.
>
> Either way, there was a tremendous lack of true creativity. We were missing lots of potential because actually that ex-player had an enormous amount to offer, but he wasn't truly involving me even though I was at the sharp end of what was going on.

When Whitaker himself was asked to coach the English hockey team, he vowed to adopt a different approach, which involved players in coming up with their own suggestions for improvement when they fell below their best performance. 'I vowed I would coach in a different way, that I would truly try to involve the guys who were on the field in the coaching, so that instead of telling them how to play I would ask them what was going on. To start with I didn't do it as well as I can now because I had no role model. There wasn't a coach who did it that way. I was on my own.'

Whitaker's basic approach to coaching was that he had to enable the players in his charge to 'go beyond where I had been. If you always hold on to the view that they can't do it as well as you could, you're always going to have a power and control issue; you're never going to let them develop because you're going to be frightened they will become better than you.'

He cites an example:

> We have players in hockey who can hit the ball very hard, but they may not be hitting it as well as they could do. I as a coach could get heavily into technique, but I haven't really got a great deal of credibility in their eyes because they can hit the ball much harder than I can. So I ask them to

think about their technique. The chances are if they're a good performer they've got the technique sorted out. There's something else going wrong.

I would coach around the areas: 'What happens when it goes really well?' and use that as a model and check what's going on now. How close is it to the ideal? What happens then is that they self-correct just by raising their awareness of what goes on when they perform really well.

The parallels with business are obvious but no less important for that. Managers who coach by telling subordinates what to do limit their trainees to a level of accomplishment no greater than the managers themselves can achieve. That level may be very high but it still imposes an unnecessary constraint and reinforces the manager's power. Managers who coach by asking questions which facilitate trainees' own learning are relying on their process skills, not their experience or their technical knowledge. As Whitaker makes clear those process skills can be developed.

GROWING SKILLS

Whitaker, who was director of coaching for the English Hockey Association from 1985 to 1989, applies a similar approach when coaching business people. It mainly involves asking a series of questions which draws out the manager's own ideas of the goals that need to be set to tackle problem areas. The coaching sessions are structured around the acronym GROW (Goals, Reality, Options and Will). The person being coached is helped to determine the goal to be achieved. The reality of the current situation is established and the options for achieving the goal examined. The will to achieve the goal is then created by committing to an action plan.

The theory is brought alive by physical activities such as races between groups participating in the training roped to wooden planks to demonstrate the importance of teamwork.

The venue for such training is often prestigious national sports centres like Bisham Abbey, where participants might come across the English soccer team in training with their manager. Whitaker admits that rubbing shoulders with international sports celebrities is part of the attraction, but argues that the link between sports coaching and improved business performance is far from superficial. Once learned, performance coaching can be practised continuously on the job, unlike many training techniques which are soon forgotten once the participants return to the work environment.

This is a view endorsed by Wigston of Barclays. 'I think it is true not just in sales training but in training as a whole that unless you are reinforcing the training message via a coaching approach back in the work place, a big part of the training spend is actually going begging because it is left at the training centre rather than applied back on the job.'

Coaching then provides managers with a means of developing themselves, of reinforcing and extending more formal training sessions, and of continuous on-the-job improvement. It may also involve a change of venue, a shift of activity, and an opportunity to talk about it. All of which would serve to associate it with a degree of excitement and glamour missing at in-house training sessions.

CONFIDENCE

Dr. Penny Hackett, company training and development manager at shoe firm Clarks International, which has so far put some fifty of its senior and middle managers through a coaching programme run by Performance Consultants, says that the rapid performance improvement achieved in the sports activities builds up confidence in the participants. This is a definite plus when the managers try to apply the theories back in the work situation, which tends to be a much longer process, requiring considerable faith and patience.

Over the past three years ICI has sent around 150 first-line managers from its maintenance division at the chemicals and polymer plant on Merseyside to learn coaching as part of an empowerment programme aimed at making its shopfloor workers more self-reliant. The tailor-made coaching programme, spearheaded by David Hemery, involves golf, hockey and grass ski-ing to drive home the message.

Joanna Cooper, ICI's central maintenance group manager at

Merseyside, believes that supervisors and other front-line managers are the key to drawing out the potential of shopfloor workers and making them more responsible and accountable for the tasks they do. 'If you believe in empowerment and you're actually trying to develop the weekly staff (shopfloor workers) to take on more responsibility and to get them to think more for themselves and rely less on decisions being made for them, that needs the role of the first-line manager to change.'

The ICI programme is built on the theme that 'a leader or coach should first generate awareness. It's through the generation of that awareness that you get the individual to take on responsibility and more accountability for the task. The individual is therefore much more likely to be interested in it and enthusiastic about it and more likely to deliver it,' suggests Cooper.

The approach has led to significant cost reductions. 'We are more effective in terms of our maintenance effort. We do more with less people,' says Cooper. 'We are at the moment starting to take out a layer of management which is very much the result of being able to grow from the bottom up.'

An 'enhanced weekly staff role' has been introduced at Merseyside, which Cooper claims would not have been possible without the coaching approach. The shopfloor workers are being given clear accountability for a particular task. 'The supervisors are standing back much more, actually operating as coaches, which has enabled us to take out this layer of management within our maintenance work. That's really taken off and brought some very significant benefits to the organisation. The weekly staff people are actually behaving very differently – not in all cases, but there's a tremendous amount of evidence that it is working.'

Clarks International, the Somerset-based shoe firm, has opted to introduce its coaching programme at the senior and middle levels of management. It initially focused on its retail operations, but there are plans to spread the approach across the board. It is part of some wide-ranging changes in management style at the shoe firm 'not only of manufacturing, but of the way we operate the business as a whole,' explains Dr. Penny Hackett. 'We have what we call the world class approach – a continuous improvement process, putting the consumer very much at the pinnacle of the pyramid.

> Coaching is not a one-off that is going to solve all the problems. It's something we are trying to integrate into the vision of the nature of the role of management. It is also part of moving the business forward in a direction that is really going to help bring out the potential within the work force that we've currently got.

Coaching is a valid and powerful technique whether it is conducted by shopfloor workers, by first-line supervisors, by senior managers or by international sportsmen. By placing the responsibility for learning on the trainee and relating it to immediate work place issues it develops confidence whether the trainee is a senior manager being coached to coach or a shopfloor worker developing financial skills.

A NEW APPROACH TO POLICING

It is not just commercial organisations that are turning to sports coaching methods to step up their performance. Apart from the military, it would be hard to think of an institution more entrenched in command and control management than the police service. But faced with a spiralling crime rate and inadequate resources, it too is seeing the sense of playing a different game.

John Whitmore, who lectures on coaching techniques at the senior police staff college at Bramshill, points out that the police are 'very visible at the moment' and 'very sensitive to public criticism. Crime is on the increase and budgets are getting smaller.'

He also notes that junior police officers can expect to find themselves in situations where they have to take personal initiatives beyond the normal accountability of their rank. 'When a bomb goes off, a twenty year old constable can find himself in charge simply because he's wearing a police uniform. The capability has to be built in for young police officers to take on that sort of responsibility.'

Kent County Constabulary has been using sports coaching methods to encourage lower-rank officers to generate innovative ways of increasing the crime detection rate, among other things.

Some 350 officers and civilian managers have undergone training in coaching. Over a thousand of the 3,000-strong force are civilians. All officers of the rank of sergeant and above are going through the coaching scheme. A main impetus for the programme has come from the fact that several layers of management were removed from the structure of the Kent police force as part of an efficiency drive. 'In consequence there was a need to recognise that the work doesn't really go away and that there is a need to have officers at all levels empowered to make decisions that reflect the policy laid down by managers,' explains chief inspector Stuart McBride, who is in charge of management and personal development for the Kent force.

McBride cites a basic example:

> If an officer on patrol is aware that the constabulary is focusing on, for example, preventing burglaries because there is a particular need for that, he can respond to calls accordingly. If he is fully aware of what's going on, he doesn't need to keep coming back and referring to his sergeant because he knows the emphasis is on burglaries.

This may seem to be an elementary part of policing, but McBride points out that it is:

> a question of formalising it and getting away from the idea that the boss is the one who knows; he has all the information and controls everything and tells everybody where to go. It's saying that the boss will be better employed perhaps at looking at the mid- and long-term future and allowing his staff to get on with the nuts and bolts of what they do – recognising that in giving them that additional responsibility, they actually enjoy the work more and respond better.

DEVELOPING AT THE INDIVIDUAL'S OWN SPEED

Coaching, in McBride's view, facilitates this radical shift in the way policing is managed:

> What I like about the coaching approach is that the coach or manager, through asking questions, if it's appropriate at a particular time, can allow the individual to develop at the individual's own speed in the direction the individual wishes to go.

In the police service there are all sorts of jobs, some of which are not crucial, some of course absolutely crucial. You wouldn't put a rookie into a firearm situation. That's obvious, but there are many ways you can say to a person, even with something as important as that: 'What would you do in such an event? What response would you expect?'

But McBride emphasises that introducing empowerment into the police force does not mean handing over complete responsibility to the policeman on the beat:

It's not true empowerment in the sense that you say 'Here's the mission statement, go away and do whatever it is you want to do'. The coach, in the coaching process, in my view, retains control and responsibility. What he does is recognise that by moving towards the empowering end of the scale people get far more ownership of issues and problems, more enjoyment, more reward.

I don't mean that it is a conning approach, that people only think they have control, but they don't really. They do have control, but that doesn't mean the boss loses control. The boss has to be more aware. The likelihood is that there is more going on, more tasks being undertaken and heavier work loads being dealt with because of the process.

McBride observes that, in addition to the structural delayering going on in police forces, pressures from society at large are dictating the need to take the empowerment route:

The quality of the individual we are recruiting into the police service today is very different to the old style recruit. One shouldn't generalise, but very often the old style recruit probably would have done national service, may well have been an ex-military person – tall and upright. Nowadays the nature of the applicants is very different requiring a different management style. In society today when somebody is told to do something the tendency is to ask why.

It may be possible for a disciplined body such as ours to hang on to the old style longer than other organisations, but at the end of the day there are so many changes in society that it is really crucial we respond to them as quickly as we can. Indeed, I think it is crucial that we accept the changes as the normal course of events rather than trying to resist them. If we are not careful we will lose the hearts and minds of our people because of an inappropriate management style.

GRADUAL PATH TO CHANGE

The sports coaching approach appealed to Kent police because it represented a gradual path to change rather than a sudden lurch. McBride says coaching can be particularly appropriate when related to some of the more delicate duties the police are obliged to perform. For example, having to notify somebody that a close relative has been killed in a road accident is a task nobody would relish. It is something that has to be handled with personal tact and compassion. Each situation has to be handled according to the circumstances. There can be no prescribed set of rules to tell an officer doing it for the first time precisely how to go about it.

Coaching can make the officer aware of all the factors that need to be taken into consideration and help him to handle it in his own way. 'A police officer is probably in the job because he's socially minded, wants to help and cares about people,' suggests McBride. 'That might sound arrogant but I believe it to be true. When the officer who has undergone coaching interrelates with the person to be told about the accident, his own humanity will come through. Instead of coming across as a stuffed shirt desperately trying to remember the stereotype formula for breaking the bad news gently, he will express his own feelings and relate as a caring human being.'

The physical exercises used in the coaching programme work well in McBride's experience:

> You're looking for change in behaviour. With a physical exercise you can see it, if it's working, sometimes straight away. If you do something in management terms, you might have to wait weeks, months or even years to see a result. The only difficulty is you are asking people to make a mental jump – that if it works in a physical way it will also work in a managerial way. But most policemen are physical types and do sports, so they mostly seem to be able to make the connection fairly easily.

Some officers, however, have been sceptical about the sports coaching approach, questioning whether it is possible to teach someone to become proficient in a particular sport if the coach is not himself an outstanding player. Becoming proficient in a sport is far short of becoming outstanding. If such a large gap in performance were needed to coach in sport or in business the task of developing outstanding individuals would be next to impossible – how would you find those who were so much better than trainees aiming to become world class? Even developing a significant number of proficient individuals would absorb all the time and energy of those who are outstanding, assuming all those who are outstanding performers can coach.

RESULTS

The practical results of the Kent force's coaching programme are hard to pinpoint. McBride admits that crime detection rates have not increased since coaching was introduced, but he does see other less tangible gains:

> If you look at the actual number of cases that are being dealt with – and that's what creates the work, when you arrest somebody and have to go through all the formal procedures – then we've improved dramatically with virtually no increase in staff. We are certainly dealing with a lot more and we know our staff are under an awful lot of pressure. I wonder how well they would have fared without coaching?
>
> Having said all that, it isn't a switch that you throw. When you are in effect trying to change cultures, it's a slow-moving process that people need to be signed up to and comfortable with. I don't think there is much about this programme that people could be uncomfortable with other than those people who sit on their hands and ask to be told what to do; 'I'll do what I'm told, no more no less'. Thank God, we haven't got too many like that.

A typical early development mechanism in police training is to assign inexperienced constables to patrol with much more experienced officers with the explicit aim of facilitating a transfer of knowledge and skill and understanding of police work. This process reflects the extent to which organisations have believed in the value of coaching before it became fashionable as a management technique. It also makes it easier to highlight coaching as a management development technique because its use is already accepted and valued within the organisation.

SPORT AND BUSINESS

David Whitaker is convinced that sport and business have a lot to learn from each other. He will be coaching the English hockey team at the next Olympics in Atlanta in 1996 and reckons that he will now be able to apply some of the lessons he has learned from the business world to the sports arena.

The main lesson that being in both worlds has taught him is that the way to generate high level performance is much the same in sport and business:

> Really good performers are highly aware and they take a very high level of personal responsibility. I don't just mean elite performers. At any level of performance, in any role – when people perform really well they show terrific awareness of what's going on and what the interaction is. Awareness and responsibility are attitudes of mind. It's all about focus of attention and the choice to take on the job and see it through to completion.
>
> There's plenty of evidence that just telling people to be more responsible doesn't generate an improved performance, because people forget. The really skilled sales manager, for example, will coach his sales people through what is happening during their sales interviews – what actually happened in the interaction.
>
> It's the way you work with people so that they choose to own the task and see it through to completion. People always have a choice and they have an uncanny knack of exercising it.

Whitaker believes that coaching is a key tool for empowerment:

> You coach people until they find solutions and it need not take away the authority of the manager. The buck still stops with the manager. Sharing responsibility is not powerful enough for me. That gives the impression that I as the manager or the coach of the hockey side carry around a lot of responsibility and you can have a bit and that makes me feel better. It's not generating responsibility. I have to carry responsibility for how well they play or how the unit performs. I can't get rid of that, but what I want to do is generate in the other people the same level of responsibility in them for doing their bit. It's not just sharing it. That's too weak for me.

SUMMARY

Living in Oxford, as one of us does, provides ample opportunity to observe one form of coaching. Along the towpath, one-handedly, cycle anxious coaches usually avoiding equally or even more anxious walkers. Their other hand grasps a megaphone and their attention is directed to the eight on the river 'Stroke. Stroke. Stroke.' The crew pull and sweat and listen for instruction through the swirls of noise. Coaches in this model are infinitely more experienced than their charges and seek to imbue the crew with their knowledge and skill.

The same model can be seen in operation any Sunday morning through the winter at most council recreation grounds as coaches and parents yell continuous instruction at small children whose primary concern is to reach the centre of the moving mass of players quickly enough to apply boot to ball.

At its best this form of coaching can be inspirational – demanding and receiving more from competitors than they ever believed they could give. It can be a powerful source of achievement, refining barely formed talent to professional competence. It can be a powerful source of growth, raising self-confidence and accomplishment to a degree that individuals' whole approach to life is affected.

Yet standing on the sidelines one suspects that most competitors, like David Whitaker, learn, after a while, to screen out most if not all of this advice, instruction and occasional abuse. At that point they are left to their own resources. Some individuals, aware enough and determined and capable enough, become their own coaches and continue to improve. While more personally satisfying or less personally dispiriting, self-coaching may be insufficient to fully develop one's talents. For many it may simply offer a dead-end of discouragement and disillusion.

FEEDBACK

An alternative is available. Providing competitors with feedback to raise their own awareness of their performance gives them the opportunity to find their own solutions to the problems which they face.

Feedback may be generated by questioning so that it encourages the competitors to raise their awareness while they are performing. This may be supplemented by video or direct observation while using questions to ensure that the analysis and interpretation are generated by players. This latter approach enables players to achieve perform-ances which may be beyond that of their coach. It is also quieter, friendlier and more enjoyable for all parties.

Really competent sustained performance comes from within. The role of the coach is to enable it to bloom and continue. Whether in sports arenas or organisations coaching offers a way to continuous improvement in the face of ever-mounting competitive pressures. Both of these models can produce really strong results. Before David Whitaker's hockey competence took him to international standard he was coached in the telling mode, and coached sufficiently well to achieve that standard. The issues are whether some circumstances favour one model more than another, whether they are reconcilable, and whether one offers more prospect of long-term success than the other.

5

COACHING TO SUIT
THE SITUATION

Empowerment is a comparatively recent phenomenon in the UK and many organisations are still finding their way. A major change of approach is required by both managers and staff to adapt to the coaching style of management. This is something that needs to be learned jointly. If managers become coaches but staff do not become trainees the manager is going to find life very difficult. So are the staff. Even when both groups are committed to the same goal there are likely to be difficulties before both feel comfortable with the new relationship.

Most people, when asked what images coaching conjures up for them, would think of sports and athletics – earnest coaches working with equally earnest competitors to improve performance. Football fields, athletic tracks, swimming pools, ice rinks would all be suitable backdrops. Work situations are less likely to appear as settings for coaching. Asked to describe coaching, the most common models would imply some kind of loop around demonstration, practice and feedback (Fig. 5.1). The coach, using skill and expertise, shows how it should be done; the trainee practises the new-shown skill, and the coach offers commentary and feedback. The former may vary from the abusive to the encouraging; the latter from the descriptive to the judgemental. These images are powerful, so powerful that they shape the expectations of coaches and trainees alike. In Chapters Five and Six we explore different models of coaching and consider their application in the world of business.

There are, as discussed in Chapter Four, at least two distinguishable models of coaching. In one the coach operates from a higher

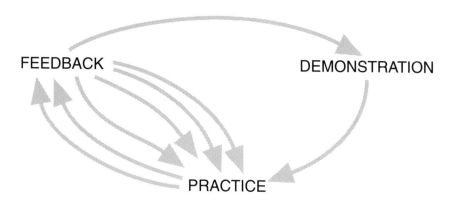

Fig. 5.1   Basic coaching loop

level of experience and skill to instruct the trainee in the best way of performing. The coach may also act as motivator, cheerleader and general enthusiast to role model the kind of commitment and excitement needed to attain results. We call this the 'expert coach' model. This is the model reviewed in Chapter Five. In the other model the coach relies much more heavily on questioning and listening techniques to raise the awareness of the trainee The coach's skills lie not in the area of technical or professional expertise but in the ability to help the trainee recognise that there is an issue, identify the causes of that issue, and generate solutions to it. This approach permits much more flexibility in responding to different individuals and more readily acknowledges that the trainee may be more accomplished than the coach. We refer to this as the 'helper coach' model. This model is discussed in Chapter Six.

Traditionally, one of the best ways to practise performance coaching was to delegate a task that stretched the subordinate and took her into new areas beyond the confines of the normal job. The pace and complexity of change now are such as to call into question the whole concept of a 'normal' job. If organisations and individuals are to remain competitive and fully employed they will need constantly to learn how to tackle tasks for which they have little or no prior experience.

It would be tempting to suggest that the 'expert coach' model applies in those circumstances where the demands of the task and means of accomplishing it are already well-established. Also, that the expert coach approach is particularly appropriate in circumstances where new staff need to be trained. But that supposes that the current methods of tackling a task are necessarily the best and that any prior experience or learning new staff bring with them is irrelevant.

It would also be tempting to propose that the 'helper coach' model is most appropriate when experienced capable staff are confronted by new problems and issues. By drawing on their existing skills and knowledge the coach enables them to find a way forward. Such an approach neglects the potential to learn from elsewhere. At Nuclear Electric, despite the substantial investments in training made by the CEGB over the years and the undoubted quality of the staff, benchmarking others' achievements was a powerful learning experience

The advantages of performance coaching as a training tool are numerous, according to Adrian Savage of Assessment Design Services, a Leamington Spa management training organisation. It requires no new resources (and therefore adds nothing to overheads); it doesn't cut across the normal chain of command; and it can be done every day, in contrast to training courses which tend to be sporadic at best and the lessons inadequately reinforced.

A PAPER EXERCISE?

Savage has helped a number of UK firms to introduce performance coaching. The system he has devised involves five stages which are encapsulated by the acronym PAPER – Purpose, Authority, Practice, Evaluation and Reflection (Figs. 5.2 and 5.3). Savage's system is a strong form of the 'expert coach' approach.

Purpose

Performance coaching should always be undertaken with a specific *purpose* in mind. Perhaps the subordinate needs to learn a particular skill. Maybe he or she needs to gain particular experience or to improve standards in a particular area. Whatever the purpose, you must be clear about it. So must the person you are coaching. Nobody should be asked to undertake any development activities without knowing the purpose and objectives.

Authority

To allow people to learn through their daily work, you must delegate full authority to complete the task. You must allow them to stand on their own feet. Delegate the necessary authority to take any essential decisions. Delegating tasks while keeping the important decisions in your own hands will not help people to learn effectively.

Asking someone to come up with a range of options from which you will make the final decision is sometimes effective, provided you can involve them in the decision or explain the outcome. This is not ideal. The best coaching situations demand that you let the subordinate have full responsibility and accept the possibility of a mistake. If you cannot allow a degree of risk, the task is not a suitable one for the purpose of coaching.

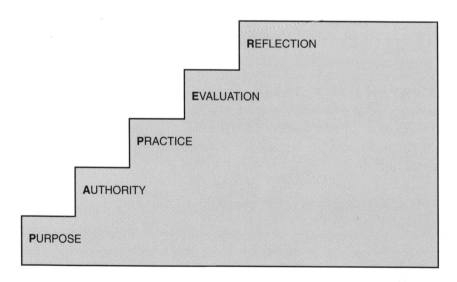

Fig. 5.2   PAPER: A step model of coaching

Practice

People do not always get things right first time. If you expect instant results you are certain to be disappointed. The coaching process will quickly turn into a frustrating and acrimonious argument. You must allow people to face a situation a number of times, learning more each time they deal with it. Practice makes perfect.

Evaluation

A coaching task differs from any other task because there is a conscious evaluation when it has been completed. To be a learning experience, you and your subordinate must take the time to consider the outcome and what can be learned from it.

It is vital that you allow your subordinate to make this evaluation. We learn best from ourselves and our own actions. People learn very little from being given good advice by others. By thinking things through ourselves we make evaluation real.

The manager's role in this process is to provide feedback. This may involve giving your opinions, pointing out things your subordinate may not have considered, explaining possible repercussions and providing praise or constructive criticism.

Reflection

People find it hard to recall large numbers of facts. It is much easier to recall a set of principles which can be applied to many situations. To derive general principles from specific actions demands reflection. We evaluate the outcome of an action, then reflect on it and discover what general principles can be abstracted and used for future guidance.

Very few situations are identical to the one in which the learning took place. If we can only apply our learning to identical situations, it will be of little use. Only by generalising a set of principles applicable to many situations have we gained a useful addition to our repertoire of skills.

The manager or supervisor has a key role in helping subordinates work through this process of reflection. You may need gently to encourage them to think about the situation by asking appropriate questions or by allowing them to explain their understanding to you.

Explaining to some other person what we think we have grasped frequently shows us gaps in our understanding. Telling other people what we have learned is an excellent way of fixing it in our minds. Above all, you need to allow people time to reflect. Time spent in learning a lesson to last a lifetime is well worthwhile. Hurrying to the next task ensures that the same mistakes will be repeated.

Using PAPER as the basis of performance coaching, Savage offers the following step-by-step approach for managers:

STAGE ONE – PURPOSE

Planning

Before you begin any coaching activity, make sure your objectives are clear. Think through what you want to achieve.

Consider the standards to be reached and any conditions you must

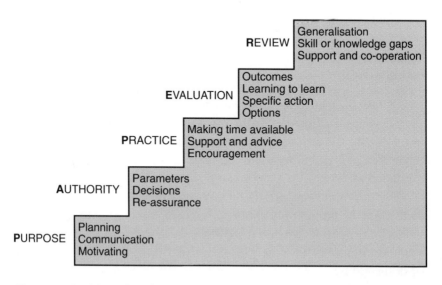

Fig. 5.3   PAPER: Coaching in steps

lay down. Decide in advance what will constitute success. Be clear on the standards that you wish your subordinate to achieve. Know what you will accept as evidence that the standard has been reached. Your subordinate may have to follow particular procedures. You may want him or her to behave in a particular way or include certain elements in the task.

Conditions are of two kinds. One condition is imposed by the organisation. This covers rules, procedures and the informal corporate culture that defines how things are done in order to be acceptable. Experienced employees will know these things; inexperienced employees may need to be told how to avoid embarrassing mistakes. The second kind is based on the learning objectives. To ensure that your subordinate learns what you want, you may need to ask for the task to be done in a particular way.

Communicating

For the task to be a learning experience, your subordinate needs answers to these three questions:
(a) What purpose do you have in mind?
(b) Why you think he or she needs this learning experience?
(c) What is the process through which they are going to learn?

Motivating

Carrying out a task with a learning objective in mind requires additional effort and thought. Take time to motivate your subordinate to carry out the task in the way you want. Make clear the benefits. Stress that successful completion will be valued. Encourage your subordinate to invest some personal interest in the task.

You cannot impose a task and expect there to be an adequate learning outcome. Imposed tasks are carried out with gritted teeth. This is not a state of mind that is conducive to learning. We learn best when we are relaxed, interested and involved. Listen carefully to your subordinate's ideas and objections. If necessary, re-define the task or the conditions to ensure that he or she is fully motivated.

STAGE TWO – AUTHORITY

Parameters

Delegate the necessary authority to carry out whatever task you are setting. Managers see this as the most risky part of coaching. You cannot take the risk away entirely; you can manage it and limit it in the interests of yourself, the organisation and the subordinate.

Do this by setting boundaries to the task. Make clear how far your subordinate can go, who else must be involved, what resources can be expended and what new or unexpected elements can be included before it is necessary to check with you. Setting clear boundaries increases people's willingness to display initiative. The message you are giving is: 'Within these parameters you have the authority to do whatever you think best. When you think you might be going outside the parameters, please come and check with me before taking any action.'

Decisions

An important element in giving accountability is to make clear which decisions are reserved for you.

The objective is to give authority while minimising unnecessary risk. You are avoiding the situation in which the subordinate takes a decision in good faith, only to find that he or she is criticised after the event. People feel that this is unfair. They respond by limiting their initiative and checking with you before taking any decision.

Reassurance

Most subordinates need some reassurance, particularly if the task you are setting them is something new. We learn best from tasks which challenge our skills and ability. We also learn best when we are relaxed. Throwing people in at the deep end only teaches them to avoid you and that part of the pool in future.

There are two stages of giving the necessary reassurance. Begin by making sure that you give a careful briefing. Point out any pitfalls that you can see; any people whom you feel must be consulted; any problems that already exist; any history to be aware of. Help your subordinate to avoid unnecessary mistakes and pass a clear message that you are doing everything you can to ensure success. Missing out this briefing stage is extremely risky. People make mistakes which could be avoided. They will also feel let down when these mistakes become apparent.

The second element is to tell people what will happen if things go wrong. Make clear that you will not punish genuine mistakes. This is the risk you are taking in order for them to learn. Explain what they should do if things start going wrong. Should they come to you? Or to someone else in your absence? Should they continue or wait for further instructions? Send them into the learning opportunity feeling as confident and relaxed as you can.

STAGE THREE – PRACTICE

Making time available

Doing a job for the first time, we are slow. Speed comes with expertise. Repetition of parts of the task will get them right. One of your important roles while people are practising is to make the necesssary time available to them. This may require you to take on some work yourself or redistribute it. It will demand patience and understanding

Support and advice

The hardest piece of self-discipline necessary during coaching is to stand back and allow the subordinate to get on with the job. Particularly hard if you see them heading for a problem or mistake. The temptation is to step in quickly with support and advice.

This natural tendency is the enemy of effective learning. You must be willing to stand back and allow the subordinate to do things in his or her own way – including making mistakes. The effective managerial coach makes clear that advice and help is always available for the asking. It is never thrust upon the subordinate when it has not been asked for.

Encouragement

If you think about a sports coach you will know what is meant by this heading. During the game the coach stands on the sideline, encouraging the team. You should do the same while your subordinate is learning.

It is easy for people to become disheartened or demotivated by their own mistakes. If we are to learn, we need to carry on, to try again, to overcome difficulties. The role of the coach is to urge us on, convincing us that we can and will do it, if only we apply the necessary energy and enthusiasm.

STAGE FOUR – EVALUATION

Outcomes

Without evaluation and feedback there is no learning. The boss's role is to help people to evaluate what they have done and learn from it. It is not to pass judgement. You need your subordinate to be honest with herself and – even more important – honest with you. Preparing the ground properly at the reassurance step will increase the likelihood of honest information.

Use questioning and reflecting techniques to help your subordinate make a proper evaluation of the task. Be ready to criticise when it is necessary. Be even more ready to praise when it is due. It is worth remembering that willingness to praise gives us the right to criticise. Subordinates are very aware of whether they are being treated fairly. Criticism from a boss who praises freely will be respected. A boss who criticises all the time is swiftly ignored.

Learning to learn

Take time with your subordinate to evaluate the learning proces as well as the task. Help your subordinate to think through what has been learned and whether any learning opportunities have been missed. Ensure that your subordinate can make effective use of learning opportunities.

Specific action

To learn we need to be able to relate specific actions to specific outcomes. If things have gone wrong we need to know the exact reasons. The evaluation stage should be as detailed and specific as possible.

This applies to success as well as failure. Do not be tempted to dismiss success with a generalised 'pat on the back'. Go through every successful stage, pointing out why it was successful. This helps your subordinate generalise and understand how to apply the lessons learned. It is the very essence of learning.

Options

Do not restrict yourself to what has happened. Help your subordinates learn more by asking them to explore the options which they rejected – or never saw.

Broaden your subordinate's outlook and encourage the ability to think through a wider range of options in the future.

STAGE FIVE – REFLECTION

Generalisation

The final stage in the process is to help your subordinates generalise from the specific actions they have just completed to other similar activities in the future. Encourage them to do this for themselves. Ask questions that will provoke them to think it through.

Skill or knowledge gaps

During the coaching process various gaps in skill or knowledge may become apparent. Make sure that you make a note of them so that you can take appropriate action.

Support and co-operation

Most of us have a tendency to want to do everything ourselves. One of the elements in the reflection process is to consider whether we would have been more effective had we sought the support and co-operation of other people.

By encouraging your subordinate to reflect in this way you are helping build effective teamworking into the organisation.

Example

An imaginary coaching session involving the delegation of a new assignment to a member of staff in the property department of a UK subsidiary of a large US multinational company illustrates how Savage's approach can be applied. The staff member (Jean) is being coached by her department head (DH):

Purpose

DH: Thanks for dropping by, Jean. I would like to go over the details of an assignment I hope you will take on for me. Head office has asked me to reduce office space overheads by twenty per cent as part of a cost cutting exercise to counteract the impact of the recession. I would like you to do a review for me of our seven offices in the UK and come up with some recommendations on where the cuts could be made. Is that a project that appeals to you?
Jean: Yes, I'd like to have a go at it.
DH: Although you have only been in the department for six months I have picked you because I think you will be more objective than any of the others. Most of them have been working here for a number of years and have built up strong relationships with other departments.

That could cause some problems when it comes to making unbiased choices. You wouldn't have that problem.

Jean: That makes sense.

DH: I think this project will also give you an opportunity to try out your people-handling skills. People are very jealous of their office space. Although we have a fair bit of open planning, people are still very possessive about their piece of territory and the amount of space they are allocated is still regarded by many of them as a reflection of their status. You will have to be careful not to ruffle sensibilities.

Jean: I can see I shall have to tread carefully.

DH: A twenty per cent cut is quite a lot. It may mean closing down one of the offices altogether and moving the staff elsewhere. Another alternative is to introduce more teleworking. Some people will probably be less reluctant to give up space if they know they are trading it in for the opportunity to work part of the time from home.

Jean: Are you expecting me to come up with a complete plan or simply to recommend where I think the cuts could be made?

DH: I would appreciate as complete a report as you can make it. I would like a good overview of what the current position is and recommendations of how to make the necessary changes. I have been given three months to file a report to head office. So if you could let me have your views in two months I would appreciate it. I suggest we meet once a fortnight to review progress and to discuss any problems you may have encountered.

Jean: Fine.

DH: I shall be very interested to see how you get on. This project will require you to practise a lot of the skills that are constantly needed in this department. As you know, there is a possible promotion in the pipeline. If you do well on this I should be able to consider you for the vacancy instead of going outside the company.

Jean: I'll do my best.

DH: It will also give you an opportunity to use some of the stuff you have learned about statistical analysis on that course you've been attending at the local college of further education.

Jean: That's right. I have also been taking lessons on the word processor. I hope by then I shall be proficient enough to type this up for you using some of the fancy graphs our new machine can produce.

DH: Sounds good to me. So do you feel happy about taking it on?
Jean: Sure. I think it will be good experience.
DH: Good. Here's a copy of the memo from head office outlining what they're after. Is there anything else you need to know?
Jean: I don't think so. You've given me a good idea of what you're looking for. If anything else occurs to me I will get back to you.
DH: Fine.

Authority

DH: By the way, this will of course involve you in crossing over into other departments where you have no authority as such. But don't worry about that. I have already spoken to the heads of departments and told them what you will be doing and that it is a high priority project for head office. They have assured me they will alert their people.
Jean: That's a help.
DH: And because of the relatively tight deadline I've given you, you may need urgent access to some of company resources – priority time on the central computer, for example. I have warned people this may be the case, but if you run into any difficulties getting what you need, let me know and I will sort it out.

Practice

(DH and Jean meet for a progress report two weeks later)

DH: How's it going?
Jean: Could be better.
DH: What's the problem.
Jean: Mainly rumour. Word got around on the grapevine before I even started that people were going to be turfed out of their offices and pushed into cramped conditions. You can imagine the resistance I encountered with that rumour circulating.
DH: Well, we can't hide facts. This will be quite a shake-up for some people. Have you been obstructed in any particular department?
Jean: The training people are giving me a bit of a hard time. I was

trying to find out how much time they actually spend at their desks and how much time away running off-site courses etc. A previous survey indicates they are only in the office about thirty per cent of the time. That's a pretty low occupation rate in an expensive building like that. It occurred to me there could be some desk sharing.

DH: Did you tell them that?

Jean: Not exactly, but they saw themselves as a target.

DH: So they've been reluctant to give you the information you need?

Jean: To some extent.

DH: Do you want me to intervene?

Jean: I don't think that will be necessary. They seem to be coming round. I pointed out there were some other options coming out of this exercise – including the fact that some categories of employees might be able to spend more time working from home with only occasional use of the office.

DH: Did that have any appeal?

Jean: I think it delivered the message that positive things as well as negative could come out of this exercise.

DH: I've had a complaint from the head of administration that you've been putting the fear of God into some of their people.

Jean: Yes, I heard they had over-reacted a bit.

DH: I told Maureen that you had a job to do and that it was up to her to calm her people down.

Jean: Thanks. I don't think there will be a problem in future. I have decided that I need to give a small presentation to each department before I start on the research, outlining the positive side of the exercise and to allay their worst fears, rather than just turning up and giving fuel to the rumours just by my presence. I think once people are fully in the picture about what I am doing, I will get the co-operation I'm after.

DH: Good. Any other problems?

Jean: I had a slight altercation with the computer department. I told them I needed to run some data through one of the computers as a matter of priority and they told me that everything they do is priority!

DH: There's probably some truth in that. I'll have another word with them and tell them this is TOP priority.

Jean: Thanks.

DH: So are you still confident about meeting the deadline?

Jean: I think it should get easier now I have learned from my mistakes. I'm still quite hopeful.

DH: That's good news. But if you look like falling behind let me know right away and I might be able to drum up some help.

Jean: I hope that won't be necessary.

DH: So do I. We're short staffed at the moment, but it's very important we meet the deadline.

Jean: I understand.

Evaluation

(Jean has finished the report reviewing office space requirements and made some recommendations. She completed it to deadline and she and her departmental head meet to discuss the implications.)

DH: First of all, thanks for getting this report to me on time, Jean. I know you ran into a lot of flak and it hasn't been easy. I am very relieved to get it because head office will be breathing down my neck if I don't deliver it on time.

Jean: I had my doubts about whether it would be ready on time, but it's surprising what you can do if you really put your mind to it.

DH: I haven't had a chance to study it in depth, but I can see you have done an excellent job in evaluating the current situation and what the impact of a twenty per cent cut in office space costs would mean. You have also come up with some interesting recommendations.

Jean: I can't claim credit for all of those. I had a brainstorming session with the rest of the property team and it's amazing how many ideas you generate when you put a lot of heads together.

DH: Some of them are pretty radical, but it's a good idea to look at all the options.

Jean: Yes. I didn't see it as my job to come up with the definitive answer. I am sure there are considerations that I am not fully aware of that will need to be taken into account, but given my present knowledge I thought you would be interested in a menu of ideas.

DH: Yes indeed. You are right about the constraints. For example, you have suggested a fairly major switch to teleworking, which would certainly free up a lot of office space, but I think you may have overlooked the fact that the technology to make that possible is itself very expensive. We need to be careful that we aren't jumping out of the frying pan into the fire.

Jean: That had occurred to me but the time factor didn't allow me to assess that in any detail.

DH: We could be cancelling out any savings by a different set of costs. I will have to look into that carefully. But you don't need to worry about that. You've done your part of it and I am very pleased with the way it turned out. We've got some valuable data to work on here and I think you learned a lot in the process.

Reflection

(DH and Jean meet again a few days later to reflect on the project as a learning exercise.)

DH: Jean, I'd like to reflect for a few moments on what you personally gained from the office space project. What did you most enjoy about it?

Jean: The best part was that it took me into other departments where I could talk to a broad range of people and get an overview of how all the different sections knit together. I am sure that will help me to see things in proper perspective in future.

DH: Yes and it also put you wise to the fact that we operate in a fairly delicate area. Office space is something people take very seriously.

Jean: That's true. I'm afraid it must have looked as though I rushed in where angels fear to tread when I first started, but I think I learned from my mistakes pretty quickly. I don't think there were any hard feelings by the time I had made it clear to everyone we weren't going to make cuts just for the sake of it. In fact, I made some contacts with people that I have followed up socially. I have been invited to join the company tennis team, for example.

DH: Good for you. What was the worst aspect of the project?

Jean: Pressure of time I suppose. I'm afraid I am not very good at working to deadlines. I have trouble organising my time.

DH: Maybe we ought to think about a course to take care of that.

Jean: I could certainly do with some help in that area.

DH: Well, you delivered the goods. That's the important thing. This project has given me an excellent idea of your capabilities. I have handled this sort of job myself in the past, but I really want to share some of my workload, particularly if it helps to stretch the members of my team.

Jean: I'd be happy to take on anything else you have that you think I could handle.

DH: I'll bear that in mind.

Jean: I really appreciate the faith you have shown in me. I realise you must have felt you were sticking your neck out a bit giving me such a delicate assignment so soon after my arrival in the company.

DH: I did have one or two sleepless nights I must admit, but nothing ventured, nothing gained.

NOT BEING NICE

Savage strives to get across three important aspects of performance coaching to the companies he advises:

> One is to make clear that coaching is not about being nice to people. It's not about having a welfare officer type of role. Coaching is about getting the job done better by your subordinates. Secondly, I try to show them that delegation is in fact the principal tool of coaching, because it is no use sitting down and talking to someone like a Dutch uncle if you never allow them to do anything. Most people learn by doing much more than by listening. Thirdly, I try to make it clear that there are an enormous range of times in which you can delegate but you, the manager, stay in control.
>
> This is the bit that frightens people, because delegation is often represented as all or nothing – the empowerment literature is a good example. You're either a nasty autocratic dictatorial kind of manager who never allows anybody to do anything at all or you are one of those wonderful empowering, transformational leaders who doesn't appear to do anything except wander around in a sort of pink haze of charisma. Most managers are concerned about control because they're held accountable.
>
> You've got to convince people that they can control it, so you start in a

small way. You maybe start delegating on a reasonably consistent basis with people you know you can trust.

The difference between delegating simply to get the task done and delegating with the aim of developing your subordinate is all to do with intention. In the case of the former, the subordinate is set a task within a given time frame and either succeeds or fails to perform, in which case he or she will receive the approval or disapproval of the boss.

If you delegate in order to develop someone, on the other hand, you are using delegation as a coaching tool. You have to make the time available to sit down with the subordinate to talk about what has been learned from the exercise, whether it was done well or badly. A lot of managers will claim they don't have the time for such in-depth analysis. But a short-term sacrifice can lead to a long-term advantage. Once subordinates start to master the higher level responsibilities you steadily pass on to them, you will find your own work load reducing to the extent that you can concentrate on the strategic issues you are really there to tackle. Once subordinates become skilled and you can trust them with higher level decisions, you can start to adopt more sophisticated techniques like management by exception.

TELL AND ASK

Savage's model is designed to enable managers to begin to make the transition from command and control to coaching. It does this by retaining managers as the source of experience and expertise and addressing their concerns about possible loss of control while making clear the need to allow trainees to find out for themselves, even if this involves making mistakes. It emphasises the power and control of the coach over the trainee. This is not a partnership of equals. This is superior to subordinate. Coaching in this way is not designed for empowering organisations. Savage is dealing with organisations with a history of centralised command and control which are beginning to melt-down in the heat of an increasingly competitive world. Pressures of work, including demands from above, coupled with an increasingly educated work force are encouraging managers to reconsider their approach to delegation and its achievement through coaching. The framework remains that of a command and control organisation.

Savage's performance coaching formula attempts to build the confidence of the subordinate by giving her her head and allowing her as much say as possible in how she will carry out the task. But this approach recognises that, depending on the skill and experience of the subordinate, there will need to be a certain amount of instruction. The subordinate will sometimes have to be told where she is straying from the straight and narrow and advice will often be needed to help the subordinate get back on track.

Some coaches, particularly sports coaches, would argue that there has to be a demonstration and practice element to coaching, commonly known as drill or instruction. Such instruction may concern the coach's view of the best way to hold a golf club or a cricket bat in the light of years of experience. Equally managers might argue that there is a best way to carry out a particular task and it is a waste of time and energy not to instruct people in that technique or approach. It is this reliance on the coach's knowledge and experience which distinguishes the expert model from the helper model of coaching.

SITUATIONAL LEADERSHIP MODEL

Coaching is not necessarily suitable for all management situations. American management experts Paul Hersey and Kenneth H. Blanchard have developed a 'situational leadership' model (Fig. 5.4) that attempts to match management style with the 'maturity' of the subordinate. They define maturity not as age or emotional stability, but as a desire for achievement, willingness to accept responsibility combined with competence and experience in relation to the complexity of the task.

The US experts believe that the relationship between manager and subordinates moves through four phases – a kind of life cycle – as subordinates develop and 'mature', and that managers need to vary their leadership style with each phase. Those two ideas – that there are different and appropriate styles of leader and that the manager, by her own interventions with her staff alters the situation she faces – are of critical importance. They create a dynamic in the manager–subordinate relationship which is driven by the manager's perception of the subordinate's maturity.

In the initial phase, when subordinates first enter the organisation, a *directing* mode of leadership is most appropriate. Subordinates have to be instructed in their tasks and familiarised with the organisation's rules and procedures. At this stage, a non-directive manager causes anxiety and confusion among new employees. However, a participatory employee relationship approach would be unsuitable at this stage because subordinates cannot yet be regarded as colleagues. In coaching terms this is akin to a straightforward instruction or drill style of interaction.

As subordinates begin to learn their tasks, a directing style of leadership remains necessary, because they are not yet willing or able to accept full responsibility. However, the manager's trust in and support of subordinates can increase as the manager becomes familiar with them and wishes to encourage further efforts on their part. This is the stage at which the American experts advocate a *coaching* style of leadership. This is perhaps closest to the popular conception of a coach – simultaneously offering instruction and encouragement to motivate and make possible higher performance at the same time.

In the third phase, subordinates' ability, motivation and desire for achievement have increased and they actively seek greater responsibility. The manager no longer needs to be directive. At this stage the manager should adopt a *supportive* leadership style. Believing in the 'best way' of tackling a particular task the manager and subordinate both accept that, once she has mastered that 'best way' no further performance development is possible or required.

As subordinates gradually become more confident, self-directing and experienced, the manager can reduce the amount of support and encouragement. By this time subordinates are ready to act on their own initiative and no longer need or expect a directive relationship with their manager. The manager can now delegate to her staff confident in their willingness and ability to cope with their tasks.

The main attraction of the situational leadership model is that it

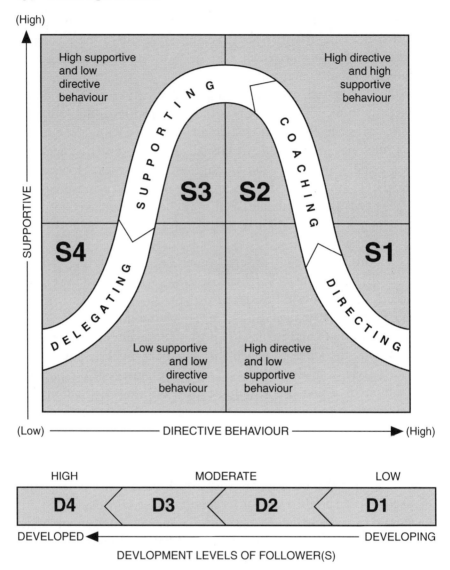

(High)

SUPPORTIVE

High supportive
and low
directive
behaviour

High directive
and high
supportive
behaviour

SUPPORTING

COACHING

S3   S2

S4   S1

DELEGATING

DIRECTING

Low supportive
and low
directive
behaviour

High directive
and low
supportive
behaviour

(Low) ——————— DIRECTIVE BEHAVIOUR ——————→ (High)

HIGH   MODERATE   LOW

D4   D3   D2   D1

DEVELOPED◄——————————————— DEVELOPING

DEVLOPMENT LEVELS OF FOLLOWER(S)

Fig. 5.4   Hersey and Blanchard's four leadership styles

recommends a dynamic and flexible approach to managing and delegating. The motivation, competence and experience of subordinates
must constantly be assessed in order to determine which style combination is most appropriate. Hersey and Blanchard argue that if the

most suitable style is applied at each phase of development it will not only motivate subordinates; it will also help them to move towards maturity in the job.

CAROUSEL

Sainsbury's, the major retail group, subscribes strongly to the situational management theories of Hersey and Blanchard and recognises that coaching is not appropriate in all business relationships. Says Judith Evans, director of corporate personnel:

> There are many frameworks for coaching and we believe you have to respond to a situation. If someone is very inexperienced, there is no point telling them to have a go and see how it works out. You need to train them first. So we have always had a very heavy investment at the beginning of people's careers into basically telling them how the job should be done. Moving on from that, we see coaching as the next phase. Once we've got people to understand the basics of the job, how do you help them to move forward in terms of increased performance?

Around 120 of Sainsbury's 200 senior managers have undertaken courses to improve their coaching skills. At the middle management level, there have been two pilot courses involving forty people out of a total population of a thousand. Many more are likely to take part over the next four to five years.

Around 300 branch managers have taken part in a programme called *Leadership Through Teamwork*, which incorporates coaching techniques. Some hundred newly-appointed supermarket managers have also been trained in coaching over the past three years.

The training basically looks at coaching from two angles – how to coach well and how to recognise the most appropriate circumstances in which to apply coaching. 'If you've got a fire in the back warehouse, it's not the time to practise coaching,' insists Evans.

On the leadership development programme, participants identify situations where they want to see change in behaviour. A 'carousel' exercise is used to illustrate in a graphic way the situational management theories of Hersey and Blanchard.

Participants identify typical situations they encounter at work and these are simulated by role playing in a series of rooms. As the participant moves through the rooms he or she encounters a situation which needs to be resolved. In one room the participant is expected to adopt a directive style; in the next a supportive style and in the next a coaching style. By having to switch from one style to another in quick succession, the participant experiences in a dramatic way the different impact each can have in dealing with a real life work situation. It is a kind of Hersey and Blanchard physical assault course and has been likened to the popular *Crystal Maze* TV programme where contestants go from room to room tackling a series of puzzles that have to be solved within a given time frame.

FIRE!

Clearly there are occasions when a coaching style of management would be singularly inappropriate. A fire on an oil rig, for example, is hardly the occasion to enter into a debate on how best to put it out. A well-practised drill is called for, which tackles the emergency with speed and efficiency.

BP Exploration faced an interesting paradox after the government report on the Piper Alpha disaster in the North Sea was published. Publication coincided with a new thrust towards empowerment at BP, which was encapsulated in the acronym OPEN (Open thinking, Personal impact, Empowerment and Networking).

The government report made a point of stressing that offshore installation managers, the people responsible for oil platform operations, should demonstrate their ability to operate in a command and control fashion in the event of an emergency. Says Tom Standing, BPEX's head of organisational development, 'Command and control is the bad guy. There can't be command and control; it's got to be open. Yet here was a government report demanding that we have a command and control capability. It was an interesting juxtaposition, but what we have been able to do in the North Sea is look at it in terms of situational leadership.'

BP takes a situational management approach to coaching. Says

Standing, 'One of the leadership skills is diagnosing the situation and the maturity of the team or the person – knowing when some specific help is needed versus when a coaching style is needed. It isn't that you're a coach all the time. You have to be able to bring it into play when it's necessary.'

An outbreak of fire is hardly the moment to begin debating the fire drill. But designing appropriate procedures to be followed in the event of fire is a task through which a team could be coached with the added advantage that having designed it they would be even more likely to follow it and the appropriate sets of instructions in an emergency.

COACHING FOR ALL SEASONS

Hersey and Blanchard offer a dynamic model to enable leaders to switch behaviours in response to staff needs. Savage offers a detailed formula to enable managers to delegate more and remain effective. In both cases staff are seen to grow and develop from the interactions. Both then offer forms of coaching. Both fit comfortably into command and control organisations which are keen to develop their staff. In Chapter 6 we explore the 'helper coach' model in more detail.

6

CALAIS LOOP AND OTHER MESSAGES

If PAPER provides an example of the 'expert coach' model, what of the 'helper coach'? Drawing on our research and experience with the Manager as Coach programme designed and delivered at Ashridge – initially for a large pharmaceutical company and later adapted as a generally available open programme – we would suggest a different approach. Following the common consultancy approach of favouring acronyms, ours is 'CALAIS' or, more fully, the 'CALAIS loop'.

The 'helper coach' model does not ascribe technical or professional superiority to the coach. What it requires of the coach is a desire to help others' development, a capacity for intelligent questioning, listening and non-evaluative feedback, and sufficient humility to be delighted and show it – when people solve their own problems and take all the credit.

This form of coaching is not dependent on status; it may be practised between colleagues, between subordinate and superior or vice-versa; or outside the workplace in any circumstances where people want to improve their performance. It specifically does not see coaching as an integral part of delegation. Delegation reflects elements of the command and control type structures. Delegation implies that staff are only permitted to do those things specifically allocated to them by their managers. In competitive environments what is needed is that staff are ready, willing and able to do whatever is necessary to meet customer needs within the framework of the overall business strategy. The CALAIS loop allows even self-managed teams to develop themselves to achieve ever higher levels of performance.

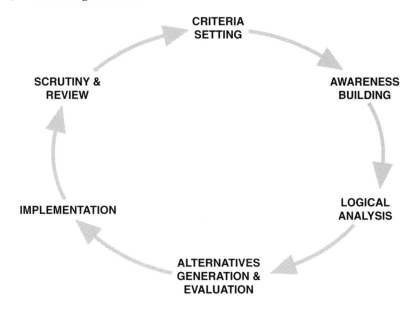

Fig. 6.1   CALAIS loop 1

THE CALAIS LOOP

The CALAIS loop comprises six stages and an indefinite number of repetitions as the trainee seeks to develop and extend his performance. The six stages are:

Criteria setting
Awareness building
Logical analysis
Alternatives generation and evaluation
Implementation
Scrutiny and review

CRITERIA SETTING

In working with trainees the key starting point is the identification of criteria relating to the developmental experience. These criteria must reflect the standards and requirements of the eventual users and customers of the output of the exercise. In other words, if this is a report to the Board, what are the Board's criteria for effective reports in general and this issue in particular? The criteria must also reflect the trainee's own needs and wishes in relation to the process, outcome and learning from the experience. The trainee may, for example, have a very strong desire to tackle the problem on his own so that he can learn from his own mistakes and enjoy his own successes. Any other parties to the experience (e.g. other team members or the manager) should be approached to identify the criteria they will use to judge the success of the experience. Obviously the trainee's own criteria in relation to his learning are critical, but so are customer requirements.

It is often useful for coach and trainee to distinguish between 'hard' and 'soft' criteria. 'Hard' criteria are those which are more obviously measurable (e.g. deadlines, budgets). In the case of the ICI rig-building exercise (see Chapter Eight) hard criteria included matching the plans and staying in budget. 'Soft' criteria are more difficult to measure but no less important. On the ICI project a key aspect was that of raising trainees' self-confidence. For many managers faced by the development of self-managed teams a key soft criteria is to be kept informed, not because they wish to change anything but because it reduces their initial anxiety levels.

Encouraging trainees to set their own criteria to measure their success focuses attention on that which the trainee wishes to change. That focus in turn provides a much higher level of ownership of the experience and greater commitment to the task. It may also assist the coach by making it much clearer how the trainee sees his current position and what he would like to achieve. Otherwise coaches risk ascribing their own criteria to trainees – to their mutual frustration.

AWARENESS BUILDING

Awareness building describes the process whereby coach and trainee develop a mutual understanding of the trainee's current level of performance and the factors which influence that performance. In

sport a new coach might ask a competitor about his previous performances. He might probe to identify what the trainee saw as his best
performances and what factors influenced that. He might also ask the
trainee how he rates those performances against his potential. Similarly, in business a coach might ask about previous experience with a
particular task, how the trainee rated it; how – if at all – it was rated by
others and so on.

The purpose of awareness building is to develop the trainee's
sensitivity to the feedback available to him by raising his capacity to
describe his own performance and the circumstances in which it
occurred. Watching footballers being interviewed on television after
games often produces the 'just talk us through this one' approach
from the commentator. Some players have no need of the video
replay, they appear to have an internal camera which records their
own and others' positions, options and actions. They have a very high
level of awareness. Others, no less talented or articulate, need to
watch the replay to recall the pattern of play. To develop themselves,
trainees need to raise their awareness so they can build on their
strengths and remedy their weaknesses.

Trainees' own awareness may be supplemented from outside.
Video recordings, customer responses, appraisals, reviews, staff
opinions, are all part and parcel of the development package. Their
real purpose, for the helper coach, is not that they allow the coach to
pass judgement but that they allow the trainee to review his own
performance. Again the key feature here is ownership. Imposed
feedback may be rejected or denied or discounted. Self-generated or
self-collected feedback, drawn out by a skilful coach, is much more
likely to be acted upon.

Feedback is the essence of all post-event control systems. Awareness building ensures that the feedback is self-monitored. Over time
the trainee can significantly raise his own awareness. Over time the
trainee can switch from feedback – gathered after the event – to
concurrent observation – gathered in progress, to feedforward,
where responses are anticipated and responded to before they occur.
In this way problems are met while they are still options and before
they have become costly. After all, driving a car relying solely on
feedback would produce a lot of bumps, scrapes, injuries and

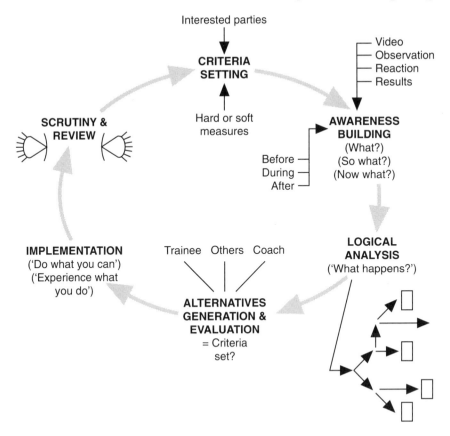

Interested parties

CRITERIA
SETTING

Hard or soft
measures

Video
Observation
Reaction
Results

SCRUTINY &
REVIEW

AWARENESS
BUILDING
(What?)
(So what?)
(Now what?)

Before
During
After

IMPLEMENTATION
('Do what you can')
('Experience what
you do')

Trainee Others Coach

ALTERNATIVES
GENERATION &
EVALUATION
= Criteria
set?

LOGICAL
ANALYSIS
('What happens?')

Fig. 6.2   CALAIS loop 2

fatalities. Anticipation has some obvious advantages.

The questioning way of coaching is not unlike the approach used in psycho-analysis. The psycho-analyst draws out the patients' own resolution to what is troubling them by asking how they feel about certain traumatic events in their life. He will offer no definitive solutions, but will merely help the patient to work through his particular emotional turmoil. In the end the patient 'owns' the solution.

The approach could also be likened to classic process consultancy where the consultant offers no expertise other than the process. The skill of the consultant lies not in knowledge or expertise but in an ability to help clients identify the issues, the blockages to progress, the options etc. 'Borrowing your watch to tell you the time' adds little value; 'borrowing your watch to help you learn how to tell the time' seems much more productive.

If the first stage of awareness building is to ask 'What?' – to find out what happened and how it is perceived by the different parties – the second stage is to move to the 'So what?' question? What would happen if nothing is done about this? If the answer is not much, then obviously very little is going to be done about it. If trainees cannot see

Feedback   Concurrent   Feedforward

Fig. 6.3   Feedback or feedforward?

strong benefits from taking a certain course of action they are not going to change the habits of a lifetime. Breaking long established habits or mindsets or responses is difficult and time consuming. Unless there are significant gains to be made the costs may appear too high.

Not getting involved, not being responsible, not developing one-self are all habits which may have been reinforced for many years. A skilful coach must draw out these issues and be prepared to confront, in a non-threatening way, the trainee with the implications of his behaviour. ICI at Merseyside and Barclays have used outdoor experiences and coaching to raise staff awareness of their behaviour and of its implications for others. Switching the setting away from work-related matters highlights current behaviour and its impact on the trainee and on others.

One of the techniques Performance Consultants uses to persuade people to assess their own performance and gain a clearer picture of the areas they need to improve is a self-evalutation rating. They ask people to rate themselves out of ten on a particular action they have undertaken. The action may be a golf swing, time management or success in turning leads into sales. In all these cases self-evaluation encourages a heightened awareness, indicates performance improvement possibilities and permits a simple self-evaluation method to measure progress. As people become more competent their standards rise, so, for those who build a real capacity for awareness, their potential performance is a continually increasing target.

At Ashridge a short powerful technique was found to be asking would-be managerial coaches to coach someone in a non-business related skill (e.g. a hobby, a card trick, etc.). Apart from providing much amusement – watching an indoor coaching session on windsurfing was unbelievable – the simple switch of context unlocked many of the coaching issues for coaches and trainees alike.

It is important that what managers offer as a coach in awareness building is not their expertise in the subject. (Many of us – including both the authors – have experienced the humiliation and frustration of being introduced to a new piece of software by an expert.) What is required from managers is their expertise as coaches. This is partly why the technique is equally effective in the sports or business arenas. Managers can, and increasingly will need to, coach staff in activities in which the managers themselves do not necessarily excel or take part.

For example, one of the authors of this book (Jim Durcan) is an ice hockey coach. He has never played ice hockey and has no particular expertise in the skills and tactics of the game to impart. Nevertheless his expertise as a coach is perfectly valid. It is possible to think of many examples where this is equally true. Film directors are not necessarily former film stars. Far more professional footballers try coaching careers than succeed. It would be rare for a conductor to play all the instruments in the orchestra.

Awareness building is one area where the expert and helper coach models diverge dramatically. In the expert model the coach is the evaluator of performance. In the helper model the trainee becomes the performance evaluator.

LOGICAL ANALYSIS

The third step is a matter of some controversy. Many coaches would argue that asking 'why' questions is unhelpful and may be counter-productive. They argue that 'why' questions tend to educe rationalisation, explanation and justification rather than progressing the learning process. As soon as you ask a 'why' question people feel obliged to justify their actions rather than think through what they are actually doing. 'Why' questions are seen as implying that the coach believes that the trainee has strayed from the best way forward. In self-defence trainees may deny part or all of the awareness they have developed in the previous phase. They may deny the implications of their actions or inactions and consequently of the need to change.

All of these are telling arguments. Embarking on the 'why' course risks a dead end. Asking 'why did you do that?' may prompt honest reflection or guardedness. Asking 'why did that happen?' shifts the focus from the individual to the issue. If the issue is poor quality then 'why did you?' sounds like an accusation. 'Why did that?' enables a discussion of production targets or supplier quality or any other relevant issue.

Of course the trainee may not initially know the answer to 'why' any more than the coach. Initial guesses may prove wide of the mark. Only a rigorous process of exploring each possible explanation and checking its validity by searching for corroborating effects will generate real understanding of the issue. A coach who operates in this style not only enables the trainee to deal with immediate issues but equips him to build on his awareness when tackling other issues.

Paradoxically the answer to 'why' questions is most likely to be found in answers to 'what' questions. 'What else was happening?' 'What happened before that?' 'What was the reaction?' Building awareness is a key stage in this process but unless the information gathered in that stage is systematically processed and understood by the trainee then he is left in a mist of confusion, uncertainty and intuition.

If a trainee is having difficulty converting enquiries into sales, asking 'why?' is likely to be unproductive, because if they already knew why they would probably have done something about it. Careful analysis of a number of enquiries – successful and unsuccessful – will allow the trainee to unlock the issue for themselves in terms of understanding the problem even if they cannot immediately see a solution.

In emphasising logical analysis our concern is not simply with 'facts' or other pieces of hard data. Emotions, feelings, reactions, and values are appropriate to the discussion. If an athlete is having trouble with his performance or a salesperson with an enquiry the problems will include issues of comprehension and emotion as well as behaviour. It may be possible to coach a child to ride a bicycle by emphasising the purely psychomotor skills involved. To coach a child to ride a bike safely involves engaging his understanding, his emotions and his values.

When the 'outage' team at Nuclear Electric's Hartlepool plant began planning how to reduce the time taken in carrying out maintenance, they had to understand the problems and difficulties which had previously occurred. If they are to meet Capp's new targets they will need to re-examine their understanding and advance it.

ALTERNATIVES GENERATION AND EVALUATION

Following the awareness building and the logical analysis, the trainee should have a sharp understanding of the nature of the problem, a clear appreciation of its causes and a real commitment to resolving it. For simple tasks these steps may be completed very quickly. For more complex problems they will take time, or risk incomplete or inadequate solutions.

The fourth phase is that of alternatives generation and evaluation. Again this is an area of debate and contention. The issue here is the extent to which the coach should draw on his own expertise to provide alternatives or solutions for the trainee. Tom Standing, BP Exploration's head of organisational development, speaks for many managers and sports coaches when he comments:

It seems patently obvious to me, for example, that if a hundred years of experience shows that holding a club in a certain way improves your golf swing, you ought to tell people that. If we go too far and suggest that telling anybody anything is wrong we shall really lose some of our efficiency. There are some solutions that fit problems that are known about. We ought to just get on with those and say: 'you wire the board that way and there won't be any shorts.'

This approach sees no virtue in allowing trainees to flounder in their own ignorance when the coach has a perfectly appropriate solution to the problem. Failure to utilise the coach's expertise is at best inefficient and at worst positively dangerous. The approach has its roots in the demonstration-practice-feedback model described in Chapter Five. Skilful coaches will minimise the demonstration aspects in order to maximise the opportunities for practice and feedback but, confronted by obvious difficulty, will demonstrate again and again with considerable patience in the hope that the trainee will learn to perform.

In contrast to this the GROW (Goals, Reality, Options, Will) model developed by Performance Consultants, outlined in Chapter Four, attempts to virtually eliminate instruction altogether. Performance Consultants, drawing on its sporting background, believes that we all have within us the ability to develop and improve to the extent that we can find our own solution to most business problems. It is only by drawing on these inner reserves that we can 'own' the course of action we take to resolve a difficult issue. As 'ownership' is a key issue in empowerment, this approach sits very well in the flexible, responsive organisation.

In a video produced by Barclays Bank in conjunction with Performance Consultants, the person learning to play golf who is taught by a non-professional learns the fastest because she is contributing to finding the approach to the game that most suits her by responding to a series of questions which 'draw out' her innate ability to find her own solutions. By contrast, the person who is told how to hold the club 'properly' by a professional coach makes slow progress because he is responding to a series of instructions and makes no personal contribution apart from attempting to carry out the demands of the teacher.

Trainees who are instructed or demonstrated to, immediately feel on trial because of the perceived need to match the instructor's proficiency. Anything less is failure. This can contribute to a negative behaviour loop where trainees will not indicate learning difficulties because of concern about looking incompetent. Their failure to indicate the difficulties means that the difficulties continue. If the instructor notices after some time, their response may reflect a degree of exasperation and deflected blame which makes it even more difficult for the learner to disclose difficulties. In one American plant coaches deliberately shifted from an encouraging style of 'This is quite simple. You'll pick it up, no trouble' to one which emphasised that it was very difficult to learn and would take considerable time. Learners learned faster with the second approach and post-entry voluntary quits dropped sharply.

Instruction or demonstration may result in the appropriate behaviour without any real understanding of why it is the appropriate behaviour. In the example Standing gives, mis-wiring the board is obviously going to create poor quality and potentially hazardous products. But if the trainee does not understand why wiring it in a different way would be inappropriate, a problem remains.

Instruction in the 'best way' neglects the reality that we are all different. A common criticism of English football is that coaches suppress individual flair and talent in favour of the 'best way'. Cricketers being coached in the 'best way' may end up worse than before because it fails to take account of their individual strengths and differences. In management development there is widespread recognition that insistence on a set procedure for handling, say, a disciplinary issue is inappropriate if it neglects the individual personalities involved.

By working with the trainee it is possible for the coach to help him identify what works best for him – even if that is different to everybody else. This process encourages active experimentation by the learner which not only makes it easier and more fun for him to learn – it may eventually produce an improvement in technique which others can try and use if it suits them.

Does it follow then that the coach's role in the generation and evaluation of alternatives is confined to questioning, listening and encouraging? No. All we would suggest is that if the coach contributes to the list of alternatives, he does so tentatively, making it clear that this is just one suggestion and needs to be treated with the same scrutiny as the rest. Quoting his experience to influence the evaluation is to cross over into the expert role.

How to choose between alternatives? Which alternative meets the criteria laid down in the first stage? Only a solution which meets all those criteria will evoke the positive feedback – internal and external – so necessary in reinforcing and confirming new behaviour. If no single alternative meets all the criteria, is it possible to combine two or more to produce a satisfactory outcome? The coach may draw on his experience at the evaluation stage to help the trainee fully identify the implications. This experience should be transmitted as far as possible in the form of open questions rather than closed ones which will be experienced as a cross-examination.

BRUISED APPLES

A simple situation found at work in the Sainsbury's context that is simulated on the training programme relates to filling shelves in a store. A store manager may find a junior employee replenishing the shelves with apples in the fruit section. He might observe the apples being dropped on to the shelves from such a height that there is a risk they might get bruised. The natural inclination of the store manager would be to intervene in a directive manner. But if he or she approaches the situation from a coaching point of view and asks the employee if he or she can see a better way of replenishing the shelves that avoids the risk of bruising, the lesson is more likely to be retained and applied next time around.

Measuring the impact of changes in managerial style is notoriously difficult, but Judith Evans, Sainsbury's director of corporate personnel, asserts:

> There is a lot of anecdotal evidence that coaching is working. The investment in the leadership programme is certainly resulting in managers being seen as more approachable and more helpful. That's not specifically related to coaching. It's related to a range of things, of which

coaching is an element.

The advantage of coaching is that you only need to solve the problem once. Once you've empowered the individual to do the job, they can do it as opposed to having to tell them again and again. The more people are involved and understand what is required of them and the more people understand the results of what they're doing, the more they want to contribute and the more likely they are to do that.

Managers may at this point feel that the benefits of this approach to coaching are all on the side of the trainee. The manager as coach is required to invest more time and energy in order to reach a situation which could be achieved more quickly by well planned instruction and demonstration handled sensibly and sensitively. An alternative way of looking at this is that managers who acquire these kinds of skills are much better equipped when called upon to coach in situations where they lack expertise or experience. It is not always the case that yesterday's best practice is still appropriate or even that the problem has been seen before. In a rapidly changing world managers are increasingly likely to be confronted by new challenges. Learning to coach using the CALAIS loop allows managers to overcome such problems and develop their staff, colleagues, customers, suppliers or superiors at the same time.

IMPLEMENTATION

Having chosen a suitable alternative all that is required is that the trainee puts it into practice while focusing on the criteria which must be met, maintaining sufficient awareness to improve next time's performance and noting data that can be used to improve or validate the logical analysis. Simple really.

The coach's role is to be on hand but not necessarily present throughout these multiple activities, to question, to listen, to encourage, to counsel and to enable the trainee to learn for himself. Telling him what is happening and why or why not undoes all the previous work. Implementation is not the acid test of coaching. It is just one more stage in the loop. If there is an acid test it is the trainee's capacity, readiness and willingness to learn. Nuclear Electric's success at Hartlepool was not just its ability to reduce the outage time. It was the development of its staff through the process.

SCRUTINY AND REVIEW

Scrutiny and review may sound like the final phase. It certainly is the stage when coach and trainee get together for the trainee to share his learning, the coach to probe and question and support and challenge. It provides a time for assessment against the criteria previously established and an opportunity to review those criteria and their appropriateness. It is also a time for coach and trainee to discuss the coaching relationship; for the coach to review his criteria, develop his awareness in the light of trainee and other feedback, to consider his own models of cause and effect in regard to his interventions and evaluate how effectively he carried out his role.

REPEATING THE PROCESS

After the scrutiny and review phase the coach and the trainee begin all over again – in the same partnership or with other people – and begin at the point of criteria identification. Because it is a loop this process can be repeated again and again. As a loop it may be positive or negative. A positive coaching loop will develop coach and trainee. Each will benefit from their association. A negative loop will lock the participants into successive rounds of painful experience, each amazed at the other's tenacity and their own capacity to absorb punishment. The difference between positive and negative loops rests in the extent to which the parties are able simultaneously to meet their objectives and develop.

CONTINUOUS IMPROVEMENT

The helper coach model might seem to work best when a new process is being introduced, as in the case of Sainsbury's installing a new computerised stocking system or the inception of semi-autonomous work units at Black and Decker's Minicraft division. In the absence of widespread experience or expertise there is little alternative other than to maximise the opportunity for personal and organisational learning. But once the new system is installed and the work groups are in place, is there enough left for the manager to get his teeth into? The expert coach model might suggest that the manager now takes on the role of coaching and maintaining best practice to ensure that the whole team matches the standards of the best. There can be little doubt that equalising performance at the top end of the range would give many organisations an enormous boost.

Alternatively, it could be argued that this is just the beginning. Given the range of competitive pressures and the instability and unpredictability of markets, organisations have no alternative other than to strive for continuous improvement. Just as the sports coach is always striving for his team to perform better in the next match, managers are anxious that their work forces should never tire in the quest for better results that will ensure they maintain their competitive position in the market place.

However good a business team's performance, they can always do better. Doing better can mean working faster, working more efficiently or achieving higher standards of quality. Most organisations would admit there is always room for improvement in these areas.

In the old days, the view was that people were taught a skill and that it would stand them in good stead for the next twenty years. Today they are lucky if a newly-acquired skill lasts them for three or four years before becoming obsolete. Over that period it will often be necesssary to supplement the original skill with a whole range of new skills that constantly need updating. Coaching provides managers with a practical way of continuously making sure that happens.

At the same time the teams they are coaching are not static. If a manager is good at developing the people who work with him, they will be continually moving on to more demanding jobs. Like the manager of a successful football team whose pre-eminence is constantly threatened by its players moving on to play for other sides, the business manager will need to be constantly re-building empowered teams to ensure that standards remain high.

These continual changes in the challenges faced and the people facing them seem more than adequate to ensure a continuing role for the manager as coach.

LONG-TERM STRATEGY

If coaching allows managers to play less of a hands-on role, it should in theory afford them the opportunity to spend more time doing what they have always claimed was a major part of their job – worrying about the long term. It is dubious whether managers ever gave as much attention to strategic planning as they wanted to do or as it needed. The reality often was that they were so caught up in the detail of operational issues that they never really got down to examining the horizon. At best it was left to the strategic planning department or, at lower levels of the organisation, treated as a special project in the hope that that would produce an answer.

Now that empowered teams are taking over much of the day-to-day detail of running their operations, managers have no excuse for not concentrating more on the long term so that they can establish the goals that give the teams a sense of direction. All our case study material makes that point repeatedly. If self-managed teams are not to go out of control or lose their way, if management is not to find itself constantly brought on board as the pilot to deal with another difficult patch, then teams must have a clear set of goals; an instantly identifiable direction.

If empowerment is to mean more than simply delegation in a command and control structure, it opens up the possibility of local initiatives, local flexibility, local responsiveness. If empowerment is not to lead to anarchy, it must be matched by a clarity of objectives and purpose. If the organisation is seen as an ocean liner there is only one bridge, one command point. If the organisation is seen as a flock of racing pigeons it needs a clear sense of direction and a stormproof means of navigation. That is management's responsibility.

CHAOS THEORY

Against that, post-modernist theories raise the question of whether there is any point planning in the long term when the speed of change is making it virtually impossible to predict the future. Managers who subscribe to the chaos theory – or simply think they are living in it – would perhaps argue even more strongly that planning is a futile exercise. But even in chaos there are some discernible patterns. The problem is recognising what these patterns are. It could therefore be argued that managers should welcome the extra time to be reflective and contemplative in order to identify what these patterns are in what is a much more complex world. It could be argued that in a post-modernist world managers need coaching skills as never before to enable each other to develop and grow although the appropriate directions for growth and development will remain obscure.

7

COACHING TEAMS

Hierarchies are out; teams are in. That seems to be the motto of many organisations today. There appears to be a veritable stampede to set up teams to replace the departmental segmentation of the now discredited pyramidal structure. This switch in some cases is a function of the move to empowerment; in others of downsizing; in others of the need to demolish departmental boundaries; in others a perception that the tasks are too complex to be undertaken by individuals; and in others a combination of some or all of these. Teams are a lot more egalitarian than departments which themselves are often mini-hierarchies based on seniority and tenure of service. In teams everyone is a team member; titles are often swept aside. There may be a team leader, but this role is often rotated or taken up according to the nature of the task being undertaken.

Teams are also a lot more flexible. They can be cross-functional, bringing together people of different disciplines in an alliance that might have been unthinkable under the inter-departmental rivalry that characterises many hierarchical organisations. That again helps to further the aims of empowerment.

There are inherent risks in passing authority down the line to front-line staff. Teams, based on the principle that two heads (or more) are better than one, are seen to have a wider range of talent and expertise than individual job-holders. A well-balanced team will contain a variety of skills and talents and ideally a blend of complementary temperaments. This very range of skill and talent and autonomy poses issues of direction and control.

Stephen Taylor, chairman of consultants Kinsley Lord, which specialises in empowerment techniques, sees the benefits outweighing the risks:

The idea, which I think is a powerful one, is that you are likely to be on better ground if you see the productive unit of the organisation not as an individual but as a team. Why? Because then the combination of the team can fill the peaks and troughs of an individual and because the strengths and weaknesses of different members of the team can compensate for each other. So a team is a stronger work entity than an individual. Therefore, rather than tasking individuals, you task a team to do something.

In some ways, it may be easier to coach teams than individuals. In most teams the mix of skills and temperaments will enable members to coach each other rather than rely entirely on the team leader. A sense of openness between team members, made easier because of the absence of status differences, may encourage a willingness to acknowledge learning difficulties or gaps in knowledge and expertise. Acknowledgement of such needs makes it easier to focus coaching in those areas. If two or more members share a common problem then they can work on it together.

Teams may also construct an internal set of checks and balances to prevent precipitous action. In theory, subjecting proposals to several people for scrutiny will provide a more thorough analysis and consequently involve less risk than individual decision making. This is particularly strong if the people are consulted on an individual basis. Reviewing proposals as a group may generate quite different dynamics. The Digital Equipment example quoted in Chapter Three revealed this other dimension to team behaviour.

Where a team becomes totally united in its convictions, if necessary by excluding dissenters as in the Digital case, it may act with more haste and less consideration than an individual would. This phenomenon of 'risky shift', of groups being more pro-risk than individuals is widely reported. This behaviour appears to be influenced by the strength of the relationships between team members and a real reluctance to cause disharmony by showing dissent, together with a willingness to screen out data which does not meet their expectations. In the Digital case, the team were aware of the likely response to their decision to cut a large part of the training programme but continued regardless. Forming strong group bonds and reinforcing each other's expectations and beliefs, the team embarked on a course contrary to that desired by the rest of the organisation. None of this is an argument against teams. It does further the case for having clearly defined goals and directions so that team members are clear about what is required of them.

ADHOCRACY

US management guru Warren Bennis, today an acknowledged authority on leadership, first came to pre-eminence in the 1960s with his prediction that bureaucracy and hierarchical, centralised control systems would shrivel within the subsequent twenty-five to fifty years to be replaced by what he called an *adhocracy* of temporary project groups. Bennis then painted a picture of the fast-moving, information-rich, kinetic organisation of the future, filled with transient cells and extremely mobile individuals, which was highlighted in Alvin Toffler's seminal book, *Future Shock*.

Executives and managers in this system would function as co-ordinators between the various transient work teams. They would be skilled in understanding the jargon of different groups of specialists and they would communicate across groups, translating and interpreting the language of one into the language of another. People in this system, according to Bennis, would be 'differentiated not vertically, according to rank and role, but flexibly and functionally, according to skill and professional training'.

Because of the transient nature of the project teams, Bennis predicted there would be a concommitant reduction in group cohesiveness. 'People will have to learn to develop quick and intense relationships on the job, and learn to bear the loss of more enduring work relationships.'

Bennis now admits that his vision of a world in which organisations are run by temporary task forces is taking longer to evolve than he had anticipated. But the tendency for organisations to do away with hierarchical structures and replace them with permanent semi-autonomous teams grouped around a particular function or customer is a revolution that is well underway. It is happening hand in hand with empowerment. Notes Sheila Rothwell of Henley Management College:

> Empowerment in practice is often empowering teams as much as individuals. The group is made responsible for a section of the manufacturing process or a group of customers, so if a complaint comes in, that group is responsible for keeping that customer satisfied and making sure that everything connected with that order is dealt with.

Rothwell makes the point that this is one of the distinctions between empowerment and the formerly fashionable concept of participation. Participation, she suggests, was a technique aimed at involving the individual more deeply in the goals of the organisation. Empowerment is a more collective approach and therefore attracts the notion that it is more advantageous to delegate to teams than to individuals.

Another distinction between empowerment and participation is that the shift to participation was largely value driven, carried forward by those who felt that staff ought to have more control over their work. Empowerment to a greater extent is customer focused; it is seen as the means of delivering higher quality and greater responsiveness while incorporating those values which drove the participation movement.

WHO'S FOR TENNIS?

According to Peter Drucker, probably the world's most enduring management guru, there are three kinds of teams whose characteristics are, or should be, determined by the work they have to do. In its July 1993 issue, *Management Today* draws attention to the American sage's latest tome, *Post-Capitalist Society*, in which he identifies different categories of teams by reference to sports. Members of a cricket team play *on* the team but not *as* a team, being assigned fixed positions as the game goes on. Soccer players have their own positions, but they all move together in a style which is dictated by their coach. Then there is the doubles pair. A small team having preferred rather than fixed positions, they 'cover' for each other with total flexibility. Needless to say, Drucker, who admits to being 'a loner' himself, puts his support behind the tennis approach to teamworking.

As a set of analogies for modern organisations Drucker's framework emphasises that there is no ideal form for a team; it depends on which game or business or market is being played. In terms of coaching, cricket teams would emphasise individual skills, including those of the captain as tactician and motivator. Coaching would be conducted from outside the team by those with appropriate expertise and experience. Football emphasises interactive skills, passing the ball involves at least two players, the form of the required interactive skills will be determined by the coach or manager who is not normally a player. The doubles pair determine their own plays and consequently choose their own coaching. Even if this involves gaining external help it is their choice. While sharing Drucker's admiration for the doubles, the issue for managers is how big is the team that can cope with that style of play. Mixed foursomes might encounter difficulties of co-ordination and collision.

BODY AND MIND

Although teams have operated in businesses for years and there are countless books, articles, courses and videos about team building and team development the issue of coaching teams rather than individuals has received less attention. Among the pioneers in the area are the consulting firm Business Bodymind.

It was sport that first took the consultancy into the arena of coaching teams to operate more effectively. The consultancy was set up in 1979 (as Sporting Bodymind) by John Syer and Christopher Connolly, two sports psychologists whose methods were based on theories developed for family therapy. They subsequently helped a wide range of sports teams, from football to pursuit cycling, to improve their performance by giving as much attention to the mental aspects of sport as to physical preparation.

Their greatest success was probably the coaching support they gave to Tottenham Hotspur Football Club during the early 1980s. During the five year period of the consultancy's association with Tottenham, it won the FA Cup twice, the UEFA Cup once and was never lower than fourth in the Football League's First Division. Their most recent success has been in helping the English cycling pursuit team to become leaders in their field, and in particular in helping to coach Chris Boardman to his Olympic Gold Medal at Barcelona.

The two sports psychologists have since applied their team coaching techniques to a wide range of companies, including Scandinavian Airlines and Ford Europe.

According to them, the mind and body are inseparable, but the mental aspects of teamwork are often neglected. In sport, there is great emphasis on physical training and fitness, but what seemed to be missing when the two psychologists first set out to explore the area, was a systematic approach to training the mind. Recalls Connolly, 'We became involved in developing training techniques and methodologies for using the mind to support and supplement performance of individuals and eventually the manager's performance as coach.'

It might be argued that in business the problems are quite different. In business team members continuously use their minds as they grapple with the flow of problems. Although the physical aspects of some jobs remain demanding, the separation of body and mind as portrayed by Connolly is largely irrelevant. A more appropriate parallel in the business context might be the divorce between business skills, knowledge and expertise and the application of those skills to team situations. It is accepted as self-evident that sports teams need to practise together in order to play effectively. A training to playing ratio of two or three to one would be regarded as the minimum for professional teams. In the business world team members are frequently expected to come together and play without any practise at all.

PROBLEM PLAYERS

Syer and Connolly were originally asked to help in dealing with 'problem players', but it soon became apparent that they had to look at the relationship of such players to the whole team and to the way in which the entire team was coached. The approach of Sporting Bodymind was that 'you can't really take a part of a functioning system and try to apply leverage on just one particular aspect of it. You won't get an individual to change unless the change is plotted within the system as a whole – in this case the team,' explains Connolly.

The issue of 'problem players' has immediate business parallels. Those who are seen as 'not team players', those who are seen to 'break the rules' in the organisation. The pattern of response is the same too. Problem business players are seen as the problem to be treated, rather than the whole set of circumstances which elicit and reinforce the problem behaviour. Making individuals more aware of their impact and of behavioural alternatives is fine, but if the pressures and behaviours around them remain as they were the individual will have trouble sustaining any change.

WARMING UP, WARMING DOWN

In 1983 Syer and Connolly published a book called *Sporting Body, Sporting Mind*, which attracted the attention of Scandinavian Airlines (SAS), which saw a possible application of the team building theories to the way their flight crews operated. Flight crews come together in an *ad hoc* fashion and work intensely with each other as they travel around the world over periods of between five and ten days before breaking up and being formed into different teams. SAS asked Syer and Connolly to help devise ways in which the flight crews could form quickly and effectively.

> We designed a programme which was basically around giving the head purser or the flight captain team building skills and then providing the team members with basic acts of agreement about the way they communicated. We began to introduce some sports concepts to do with warming up and warming down, which is part of the progressive stages a team goes through when they're preparing for a match.

This approach starts with 'warming up in the environment of the game and planning your strategy about where you are and what the circumstances are that you are going to perform under'.

Connolly was 'amazed' when travelling to sports venues with Tottenham Hotspur that the first thing the players did when they arrived for an away game was to walk around the pitch. 'They would take a walk around the pitch to see what condition it was in. As an American, I was quite surprised to discover that English pitches differ club to club – some a bit wider, some a bit longer. The kind of spaces they've got around them influences their perceptions of distance and perspective.'

This was an experience that Connolly and Syer were later to take into account when coaching business teams. They apply the same warming up features for corporate meetings. Says Connolly: 'Different meetings should have different environments – different arrangements of tables and seating depending on the purpose of the meeting – whether it is a presentation or a discussion or an interactive meeting.'

Much of the standard material on team development derives from Tuckman's model of Forming, Storming, Norming, Performing and Adjourning. The Forming and Adjourning phases could be matched against Connolly's warming up and warming down but the importance of setting and environment is often neglected. Connolly's stages are used every time a team plays, whereas in business it is often assumed that team development takes place over the whole lifetime of the team rather than as a series of short repeated cycles which occur every time the team performs.

HIDING BEHIND TABLES

When coaching football teams Connolly and Syer used to find that the manager, when he gave a talk on strategy, would stand some distance from the players who would be seated in rows in front of him. The consultants persuaded the manager to sit in a circle with the team to facilitate much more fluid interaction.

> It's commonsense really, but when we started doing it, it was quite a shock to people – and still is sometimes. You have to take tables away

behind which people hide. If they are meetings which are not to do with masses of papers and data we take the tables away. Basically when there's a meeting about conveying information they're necessary. It's when you're looking to generate ideas or planning strategies that the open format is necessary.

Business Bodymind has developed a programme to enhance the team leader's skill as a coach.

The idea is that you draw out the resources of your team rather than imposing your will on them. That ties in with our basic approach that the team is synergistic insofar as the constituent parts are able to express their potential. We are not from the Brian Clough school of management (the abrasive and irascible former manager of Nottingham Forest Football Club, noted for speaking his mind in no uncertain terms).

That approach has gone out of fashion. There was a period up to the last ten or twenty years that the manager was a patriarchal figure and led from the front. Football players are no longer regarded as children. You have to speak to the adult in them and to do that you draw out their resources rather than imposing your will on them.

The parallel between Connolly's conclusions about the role of coach and our conception of the helper coach are obvious. In both, the coach's role is that of drawing out the players' contributions rather than prescribing her own.

TEAM IDENTITY

One of the problems team leaders often struggle with, in Connolly's experience, is 'the paradox of trying to achieve a team identity that embraces common goals and a unified vision while at the same time encouraging the individuality of team members and drawing out their unique contribution to the benefit of the team as a whole.'

That paradox presents itself sharply in business where it usually surfaces as a control issue. Managers want to empower staff to use their flair and talent to the benefit of the organisation but wish to prevent or restrain too much individuality. Visionary leadership which provides a clear sense of direction and a general sense of commitment, while not predicting the terrain or prescribing the route, is the current business response to resolving the paradox.

One of the common issues Business Bodymind helps companies grapple with today is the problem of teams being set up in organisations that are downsizing or integrating previously separate departments. These teams invariably find themselves having to take on a lot more work with fewer people. In addition, people of different disciplines are often thrown together who have previously never worked together and may in fact have been departmental rivals.

In BP, for example, Business Bodymind has helped with the integration of the R&D and engineering functions under a reorganised structure. This required the amalgamation of professionals who did not always have a lot of time for each other when they operated in separate divisions. 'Engineers tend to think that researchers are fairly airy-fairy or not involved in the real world and researchers tend to think that engineers can't keep their finger nails clean,' jokes Connolly.

> BP is now realising the complications of that. So it's building a department of about 260 people, downsized from considerably more than that, in which these cross-disciplines are integrated in working teams of between eight and sixteen, where there are mixtures of functions as well as grades and that kind of thing. There again, it's very important to work with the individuals and to build a sense of what they have to offer that is unique and different and somehow integrate that into the team as a whole.

Coaching cross-functional teams, coaching temporary teams, coaching teams which do not initially respect each other's talents and contributions; all of these pose problems beyond those experienced when coaching on a one-to-one basis or those of developing more permanent teams. The current development of organisations creates situations where people are members of several teams, the composition of which vary. If these, in Drucker's terms, were cricket teams then coaching could concentrate on individuals. In reality these teams are frequently playing doubles with many more than two people.

The coach then has to find ways for the team to quickly establish or re-establish its sense of identity and cohesion in relation to the context and conditions it faces at the time. Forming the team does not just happen once when it first comes together. Forming the team happens every time it comes together. Forming the team is a key responsibility of the coach. The way she does that depends on which game the team is playing. Cricket teams require a different warm up to that of footballers or ice hockey players.

Having accomplished the warm up coaches need to find ways of engaging the team's minds and emotions constructively and positively, not just with the immediate task in hand but with their performance as a team. They need to go through the CALAIS loop with the important amendment in the criteria identification and setting stage of determining team members' expectations and learning needs in relation to each other. Handling those group dynamics will vary with the skill and personality of the coach and those of the team members. Brian Clough may have retired but there are still many coaches who want their teams to play according to the coach's plan rather than as an eleven person doubles team. In business many managers would feel more comfortable about determining the strategy and tactics and then instructing their team in the execution. In some circumstances, as with the Republic of Ireland's football team, that approach may achieve results.

LEADERLESS?

Connolly is not in favour of the concept of leaderless teams. He believes there will always be a need for an executive function in teams. In his view, it will always be necessary for someone to take the lead in making choices and decisions, but there is nevertheless plenty of room for managers to empower teams and provide them with the opportunity to operate with a considerable degree of autonomy. He suggests that there is a middle ground between the two extremes which the manager as coach needs to explore.

> Most of the middle ground involves situations where the manager consults team members about their opinions and takes decisions which may represent the general consensus of the team or may go against the

consensus of the team. If team members have a choice between not being consulted or being consulted and the manager making his own choice, they prefer the latter. If they have been consulted it's a form of recognition which is a preliminary to empowerment.

When Sherwood Computer Services created a set of self-managed teams reporting directly to the Board, it left it to the teams themselves to decide whether or not to have a leader. In any team there will come a time when an individual places an item on the agenda or pushes a discussion towards closure. Such behaviour is not the exclusive prerogative of the leader. Any team member can do so. In a leaderless team the leadership role shifts on a flexible basis, like the play in a doubles game. The notion that offering a team a choice between consultation and non-consultation is empowerment is difficult to grasp. The right to offer that choice is retained by the manager. There are echoes of command and control structures in this approach.

Connolly stresses the recognition element:

> Before you can empower people you need to demonstrate that you actually recognise and see them, because empowerment isn't a one-way process. As a team leader I empower my team members by recognising them, by delegating power and authority to them. But the recognition element is sometimes forgotten. You get managers who say: 'I empower my people. I delegate authority and responsibility to them', but they don't actually see the person. So the person may feel the responsibility, but they may not necessarily feel the recognition or the empowerment or even the self-esteem. They don't feel they are seen or heard.
>
> To use a parenting model, parents say: 'I look after my child. It has everything it needs.' But what the child really needs is a little bit of attention or affection or contact. That's another area where I think managers really struggle. They empower people in terms of authority and responsibility but they don't want to actually sit down and talk to the person, communicate with them and make contact with them, which are much more interpersonal skills.

Empowering teams involves recognising not only the individual members of the team but also the team itself as a separate entity with its own feelings, emotions and thoughts which are more than the sum of the individuals. Team coaches constantly move between inter-action with the individuals and interaction with the team.

KNOW YOURSELF

Connolly believes managers need to get to know themselves well to be effective coaches to teams.

> You need to become aware of yourself and appreciate yourself. After that, you can become aware of others and their differences and you then appreciate their differences. From that you can begin to make contact and once you make contact you actually engage in communication that is genuine and then from communication you engender respect and respect leads to trust. So there are a number of communication skills involving questioning and framing information and listening.

Sometimes, Connolly finds, there is a tendency for managers not to 'self-reflect, to look at themselves. The second aspect of that is to see how people are different to you and by using questioning and re-stating and listening and so forth you begin to recognise why an individual is different to you and where similar. Based on that you begin to plan joint strategies that include my needs as a manager and the individual's needs as a person.'

Connolly suggests that the model coaches work with should depend on the issues they are dealing with. He compares it to an electrical kitchen appliance on which can be attached all kinds of tools from an egg beater to a cake mixer.

> There are a number of tools or techniques that as a team leader you can attach to your team and your session. Some are very specific problem-solving sessions, so then we've got a problem-solving model. Others are sessions on creativity and for that we have a model with which we define, generate, refine and discriminate – four stages for generating ideas. Then we've got a standard model for planning. So you've got all these different techniques depending on the task, but in the context of the task there's the basic knowledge of what works with teams and the manager which involves: preview a session, the warm up stage, then engage in a mixture of task maintenance and process and then you warm down and you review the objectives and action steps and you end up with how that will work for

you as a person or an individual. Then you review the session afterwards – the implementation strategy etc.

As well as sensitivity to the issues, coaches also need to vary their approach depending on the mood of the team, the game they are in and the players available. In writing this section my thoughts are continually distracted by tomorrow's ice hockey game when a newly formed team take on a well-established local rival. The warm up will focus on issues of confidence, mutual support and the learning opportunities offered. Later in the season the warm up would focus on analysis of the opposition and developments from the last game.

SHIFT

Just as managers are having to make a major switch in their operating style when dealing with individuals in the organisation, so too they are having to adapt to a new mode of thinking when coaching teams. Observes Connolly:

> What you have to realise is that people have been trained to function in a certain way and that organisations have normalised team members. So that the people who have been successful in that organisation are those who have been active in a command and control function or in a bureaucratic structure where they didn't ask people's opinions; they told people what to do. So there's a fundamental shift in their relationship with team members.
>
> It's just the same sort of shift as from the Brian Clough days of football. Sports coaches are no longer telling people what to do; they are asking for input and advice and based upon that, they are seeking to get some consensus for implementation, because the closer you are to consensus on a strategy, the more successfully you're going to implement the strategy.
>
> In Japan you don't find the kind of high profile managers that predominate in the West. Personality and charisma are not seen as necessary qualifications in Japan. You only hear about a few grandfathers who founded the huge conglomerates. That's because there is a need to achieve consensus, which often means setting aside your personal views in order to make sure there's a collective team approach.

The interesting thing in my experience – which again is do with empowerment – is that provided in terms of marketing you've got the direction more or less right, teams are much more powerful implementing courses of action about which there is consensus than they are about unilateral ones, even though the unilateral decisions may be more efficient or more effective. When you get individuals mobilised around a team objective they find a way to make it work.

That means, in Connolly's view, that team leaders, or coaches, need to be visionary.

They certainly need to be setting new goals, new objectives, seeking for new ways of working and then empowering team members to carry out the tactics because they have the product expertise and knowledge. As a team leader you can't have that knowledge like you might have had it before. Things change too fast. What is necessary is to be able to hold this clear vision or direction and to make sure you allow team members to develop the tactics for implementing it. It's a question of finding the right level on which to engage people.

I've seen many team vision statements, mission statements, which hang on the wall or are plasticised and sit on the desk until they finally collect dust. These visions don't really mean anything unless you empower people with the wherewithal to implement the actual tactics.

BEING A LEADER

The kind of leader needed is an issue we will return to in the final chapter. Unlike sports teams however, in business it is common for people to be members of several teams simultaneously. If the organisation operates with clearly defined team leaders this means individuals need to make the adjustment from being leader to not being leader depending on the context. If their conception of not being leader involves being less participative, less initiating, less coaching, then it is also less empowering. The smaller the distinction made between roles the easier it is to transfer from one team to another and the more empowered the whole organisation.

Whether the leader acts as a visionary or as a motivating coach, she still has to handle the group dynamics involved in coaching teams.

Suppose the coach tries to build awareness by asking the team collectively to rate its current performance on a scale from zero to 10. In a really well-integrated team there might be real consensus. In a deflated team there may be no overt disagreement. In between individuals may seek to rate themselves or their section of the team. 'It's all the fault of the engineers.' Handling such dynamics requires real facilitative skills to move from blame and accusation to responsibility and analysis.

AN INSPIRATION

Having emphasised some of the difficulties of coaching teams it is worth recalling the pleasures. Four or five years ago an under-12 ice hockey team I (Jim Durcan) coached had a long losing streak. I worried that the players would become discouraged. But after every game the same phenomenon occurred. Regardless of the score they were bright, talkative and very committed. Talking to each other, to me and to their family and friends they recounted the progress they had made, the improvement in fellow players, the narrowing gap between themselves and the opposition. Their capacity for mutual reinforcement and encouragement was wonderful; their tolerance of each other's learning needs an inspiration. Their natural enthusiasm and enjoyment made the results irrelevant, their progress was everything.

NUCLEAR ELECTRIC

Empowered teams are at the heart of the culture change programme being introduced at Nuclear Electric's Hartlepool station (see case study at the end of Chapter Two on empowerment). A change support team has been set up to coach the members of the teams which are tackling a wide variety of issues to help the station become more productive and cost-conscious as part of its endeavour to achieve profitability without the aid of government subsidy.

A serious problem in introducing the team concept was that engineers had traditionally been hired primarily for their technical ability, not for their man management skills. Says Ian Briggs, the change agent at the Hartlepool station who is spearheading the programme, 'We made a mistake at the middle management level and one of the things we are going to have to do is move some of these people aside one way or another. Part of the solution is to give them projects that enable them to apply their real expertise. Some of them find it a relief, to be honest.'

An additional problem was the rigid hierarchy in the existing organisation. At the apex was the station manager, an engineering manager and a production manager. Under them were what Briggs calls 'silos' of engineering departments which guarded their expertise in electrical, mechanical and instrumental engineering jealously. Because of the nature of the work, engineers have always been regarded as the elite of a nuclear power station. The culture change programme threatened the bastions of entrenched working practices and to undermine the professional pride that engineers hold dear.

To help counter this problem, cross-functional teams were formed to decide how the changes could be best implemented. To break down the former rigid structure of 'silos', care was taken to ensure that each team had a mix of people from different disciplines. Somebody from the instruments section was expected to work alongside somebody from the mechanical section, alongside somebody from the canteen staff, for example.

TEAMWORK FOR PERFORMANCE

The starting point was Teamwork for Performance, a company-wide initiative introduced throughout all Nuclear Electric's twelve power stations, but mainly focused on the Hartlepool and Wylfa stations. The aim was to make people aware of the need for change and to 'unfreeze' their attitudes. Under this programme teams were formed to look at ways to improve performance. One group, for example, looked at the nature of teamworking and presented its findings to management in July 1992. Explains Keith Gorton, a member of the change support group that is helping to coach the teams:

> We set up a team to look at the concept of teamwork. We were looking for the principles behind it. We read all the books, visited different firms and the work groups came up with a list of principles and presented their findings.
>
> It was nothing revolutionary – about twelve principles, where we said if you want teamwork you should go for these and presented that to management. It gave a direction to head for. What sort of things should you tackle when you want to enhance teamwork? You need a team leader and you need team members who enjoy the same conditions of employment. None of these principles were absolute, but they all enhanced the chances of getting good teamwork.

To put these principles into practice a work group called TOR (Teamwork and Organisational Restructuring) was set up. It established four sub-groups to explore in more detail how teamworking could be made more effective. One group looked at what was required of a team leader; another at how teams should be ideally constituted. A third group looked at how existing work processes should be redesigned to accommodate the new approach. The fourth group explored the back-up support needed in terms of consultancy and training.

Says Gorton, 'we knew we had to have good team leaders. If we didn't have good team leaders the teams would fail. We knew the team members would have increased responsibilities. We knew that the current team structures and the work processes were out of synch.'

It was obvious that it would be pointless tinkering with existing work teams since these were often only dealing with a fragmented part of the whole work process, which limited their scope of action. Process re-engineering was therefore introduced with the help of socio-technical analysis, a technique that examines both the technical and people side of work flow.

Says Gorton:

> We realised that if you wanted to enhance teamwork, it was no use taking existing teams. We already have teams; some of them have quite good teamworkers. It was pointless just to take the existing teams and the existing boundaries and just work from within and try to increase teamworking, because sometimes they were doing the wrong job. Processes cut across so many different teams. Even if you re-designed the individual teams they'd still feel dissatisfied because they were handling a very fragmented part of the work process. We realised that if you really wanted a team to act in an enthusiastic, committed way, it had to have more control over the work processes.

Re-designing the fuel route

It takes time for traditions to be replaced by the new empowered approach and Briggs admits that there have been problems with getting the work process teams to operate in the new style. For example, a team was set up to try to streamline the process by which the fuel rods are routed through the reactor. (The fuel rods arrive from NFL for storage at Hartlepool, are lowered into the reactor where they burn up before being discharged and sent back to Windscale for reprocessing.)

Says Briggs:

> That provides an excellent, defined process that you can do your redesign on and that's been done now and they have identified thousands of savings on the practices we've had in the past. Now we are at the implementation stage, but we are having immense difficulties, to be honest, because we have the classic situation of the engineer believing that he is the team leader. We've said: 'No, your team leader will call you into his team on the fuel route when you're required'. The letting go process is hard.

An eight-man team was formed to explore the possibility of re-designing the fuel route process. Experience had taught Nuclear Electric that asking for volunteers was not a good idea. People tended to volunteer for the wrong reasons (to avoid shift work, for example). So the fuel rod team was hand picked and consisted of a cross-section of people, ranging from a reactor engineer to plant operators. They were first coached in the technique of socio-technical analysis by management consultants Kinsley Lord.

The team broke the fuel rod route down into twelve separate processes and applied socio-technical analysis (STA) to each of them. Explains George Cumming, a member of the change support team: 'STA shows you the relationship between the people and the job and how the job is being performed. In the end you find you've done away with people who shouldn't be there. Out of the twelve processes, five of them were all right; they'd evolved properly; they were efficient; they were effective. We couldn't change them. Seven of the processes were a mess.'

Multi-skilling

The work design team examined the other five processes by comparing the way they were currently being carried out with what the ideal might be, sweeping aside all constraints and looking for radical changes in approach. Says Cumming:

> When we started we discovered that an operator could do a job a fitter was doing; a fitter could do a job an electrician was doing. All of a sudden we discovered we were into the realms of multi-skilling, which is really a dirty word at Hartlepool.
>
> We found that if you let the fitter do a bit of the electrician's work, for example, the system just flowed from start to finish.

Nuclear Electric found that it was less emotive to talk about skill broadening than multi-skilling, which was something of an anathema to the unions. Says Briggs:

> Classically an electrician did something and then waited for a mechanical fitter to come along and sort out the next stage of the job. We are now broadening people's skills so that they can get the task finished, which is

multi-skilling if you like. For this industry that is a big step. To make it work we've got to look at traditional skills and the unions are finding it immensely difficult to be dragged along.

Adds Cumming, 'When we looked at it we found that eighty per cent were core skills, ten per cent was skill broadening. I'm not sure what happened to the other ten per cent. I think it went out of the window.'

The prospect of only having to share ten per cent of their skills was something the Hartlepool craftsmen could embrace. It did not threaten their core skills, but for those promoting the change programme it was an important breakthrough. It opened the door just wide enough to start on the road of discarding outmoded work practices.

The fuel rod route team had pioneered an important change of attitude that could conceivably be applied across the board, but it had also opened a can of worms that it could not handle on its own. The obvious solution was to set up a project group that would look at the whole area of skill broadening.

The project group set up to examine this area is exploring among other things the establishment of an on-site training facility. Says Briggs, 'They'll be designing competency-based training packages with some help from our training experts. They're going to get involved in designing the payment scheme for implementing it. This isn't the classic situation of management saying this is what you are going to do.'

Owning the change programme

The work teams are now building their own change programmes into their business plans and Briggs and his colleagues are playing a less directive role. The change support team Briggs leads is now acting as an internal consultancy to provide the back-up skills and training to equip the work teams with the tools they need. Insists Briggs, 'The teams have got to own the problem and to go out there and deliver it. What you mustn't do is take the problem off them. Rescuing is a dangerous management technique.'

Equally, it is dangerous to pass too much authority down the line too quickly, as Nuclear Electric has discovered. Adds Briggs:

The danger is that you go from directive management to delegation in one step, which is abdication. It has happened. When you move to teams as fast as we have, people are fearful because they feel they are on their own without support. You've really got to go through the coaching phase and the supportive phase (see Hersey and Blanchard in Chapter Five). Going straight to delegation confuses the hell out of people, because they say he's told me what to do but he hasn't given me any support or coaching to get through it.

Inevitable

Jack Brass is something of a rarity at Hartlepool. He is one of the old guard who not only accepts the change programme as inevitable but positively embraces it. An AEEU shop steward, who has been in the power generation business for nearly twenty-seven years, and, by his own admission, 'one of the best known faces' at the station, Brass is the kind of shopfloor worker that Briggs and his change team are most anxious to win over. Brass, who can trace his ancestry back to the days of William the Conqueror, recalls that in his early days as a mechanical fitter 'it was trespassing actually to touch the tool of another trade'.

He is now convinced that skill-broadening is the way ahead. 'I suspect it will eventually come to the point where we have no such thing as electrical fitters or mechanical fitters or instrument fitters. It will be all technicians. They will all be multi-craft, so we won't need as many men. This is where modern technology is taking us. It's moving on and you've got to move with it.'

Brass also sees the teams becoming less dependent on the supervisor for routine work. He cites the example that in the past when he was stripping down a pump and needed a spare part, he would go to his supervisor and ask for the relevant code number to order it from stores. A computer programme has now been introduced at Hartlepool which will allow him and around twenty per cent of the work force to be able to call up code numbers on screen.

In the bad old days, Brass can 'actually recall going to a supervisor, who had to go to his senior who had to go to his senior and so on up the line and it took somewhere in the region of two weeks to get a spare. Now all we have to do is tap a few keys.'

Not everyone on the shopfloor at Hartlepool is so convinced, however. Says Brass: 'As a shop steward I try to emphasise to the lads that this change has got to be. They think I'm selling them down the river.'

Brass is a member of a cross-functional team tackling safety culture at the power station. Most of the team members are rotated. This new role finds Brass sitting in an office for the first time in his career. The walls are lined with VDU screens – a far cry from the pumps and bearings of his traditional work. He quite evidently relishes the change of pace, but he refuses to swap his customary jeans and open neck shirt for the suit and tie of an office worker. He knows it would be like a red rag to a bull if he turned up on the shopfloor dressed like a manager.

Brass sees the teamworking approach as a way to 'get the work force on the shopfloor involved in management in some way'. He welcomes the fact that management now 'realises that the expertise is there on the shopfloor. They now say: "We've been administering orders for years. For years it's been: You will. Now it's: Can we?" To get this change-over going management had to give up such things as their car park. They gave up their dining room and they now eat in the canteen like everybody else. The Japanese culture is coming into it.'

Bastion

There are currently around seven cross-functional teams operating at Hartlepool, which involve people from different areas of the plant working together. In addition, there are a number of work improvement teams looking at specific areas of the plant, including a shiftwork re-design team. An engineering re-design team has also been set up. Says Briggs: 'That's the big bastion of the old culture.'

Briggs believes that socio-technical analysis is a vital tool for re-designing the organisation:

My personal view is that if you look back at Bethlehem Steel and Taylor in the early 1900s when everyone was looking at work reorganisation, the focus was on the technical side of it. You can quite rapidly, scientifically, technically analyse a process and get something sorted out. But the other side of the coin is the social side, which is how the teams are working. So I think you've got to get ownership of the re-design process by the people who do it and they'll tell you the social side of it.

ROYAL MAIL

In the summer of 1993 the Royal Mail held its fourth national 'Teamwork' jamboree at Milton Keynes. Some seventy of its most inspired process improvement teams displayed their achievements to around 10,000 visitors who attended the two-day event. The teams are a result of a major reorganisation of the Royal Mail that saw its head office staff reduced from 2,000 to a mere 160 and a comprehensive attempt to cascade empowerment to front-line postmen. Observes Ian Raisbeck, Royal Mail's quality director:

> When we did Teamwork 1990, because of the status of the cascade, those improvement project teams were mainly managerial, some of them comprised entirely of directors, but sixty per cent of them are now front-line teams. The change in emphasis has been that more and more of the teams have been front-line employees and that will tend to grow because in numerical terms there are 140,000 front-line employees.

Project teams have become such a way of life at Royal Mail that dozens of regional heats are now held every year to select the very best examples to go forward to the national event. There has also been a steady trend towards forming joint improvement projects with some of the Royal Mail's key customers.

The focus for teamwork at Royal Mail has been on 'improving what you do.' The approach has been cascaded down the vast organisation to the front line, which can be, for example, a large delivery office. Normally, a quality guidance group, primarily comprising employees, prioritises ideas for improvement and then sets up teams to implement them. Says Raisbeck:

> There is a very definite element of empowerment, but it's empowerment within a framework. It's not at the end of the spectrum where you're talking about self-managed work groups. We do intend to increase the self-managed component of the way people operate. At Deeside, for example, we have a delivery office where the manager almost completely stands back in a coach and supportive mode and they work in teams where the leader is a postman/postwoman and they do a tremendous amount in the self-managed sense.

Raisbeck favours a steady progression towards empowered teams rather than the quantum leap preferred by some organisations.

> The whole question of empowerment is the various degrees of freedom you begin to introduce, particularly when you talk about the manager as coach. This is something we emphasise in our leadership charter and our leadership feedback system. It looks at it in terms of the manager in this supportive coaching role. You progressively move the organisation to the point where people feel happier in terms not only of releasing people to operate in a different way, but supporting them to do it.

Aiming for accuracy at the Plymouth sorting office

Teams of postmen at the Royal Mail's Plymouth sorting office have been empowered to check their own accuracy by a system called In-Process Quality Measurement (IPQM). It is part of a general effort to coach the sorters to take more control of their own work while at the same time improving the quality of the Royal Mail's service. Mis-sorting and the despatch of letters to the wrong delivery points have been significantly reduced as a result.

The traditional way of checking accuracy has been for someone outside the sorting process to arrive with a clip board and take a sample of letters to check whether they have been sorted into the right areas. Says Gwyn Williams, a process support manager, based at the Royal Mail's divisional headquarters for South Wales and the South West:

> They've taken that information to a desk, done some data processing to it, often applied it to traffic figures – by that I mean the amount of work that goes through the office – to get some sort of statistical results out of it. By Day Three they may actually have got the result and they probably feed it upwards to a shift manager, someone like that. The shift manager will look at the information. If there has been a problem, he will probably feed it to the front-line manager. Five days later it might actually get back to the people who were doing the work in the first place – the postmen.

The drawbacks to this protracted checking procedure are obvious. By the time any problems with the sorting of the post have been pinpointed it is too late to rectify them. The stable door is being shut after the horse has bolted. Secondly the check has been carried out by an 'outsider', taking the responsibility away from the postmen actually carrying out the work. The person conducting the check is seen as a kind of inspector, with the express purpose of pointing out the sorters' faults and making their lives more difficult.

The aim of IPQM is to make the checking an integral part of the postmen's job, for them to take a regular sample of the quality of their work, chart it and interpret it on the spot so that if there is a problem they pick it up immediately. At the Royal Mail's Plymouth sorting office postmen in adjacent working areas check each other's work by taking samples every half an hour.

The results of these checks are recorded. Provided the number of mis-sorts is below an agreed control limit, no immediate action is taken. If however, the number of errors in a sample exceeds the upper control limit, the alarm bells are instantly sounded and the errors normally rectified before the mail leaves the sorting office.

For example, on one occasion shortly after the IPQM system had been installed at Plymouth, a sample of post on its way to Devon destinations was found to have eight errors in a batch of twenty-five letters – a level well above the control limit. The problem was flagged up to the front-line manager who immediately investigated the source of the difficulty. It turned out that the postman concerned was standing in for someone who was away sick and was not adequately trained in that particular postal area. Explains Williams:

> You need a lot of local knowledge to sort for some of these places and it was realised that through no fault of his own this person had been put on to a job that he couldn't do. So he was removed immediately and the performance went back to its usual high level. If the traditional way of checking was still in operation, that situation would not have come to light for five days.

The old checking system was more attuned to gathering statistical information than to raising the alarm when serious departures from the norm were revealed. Says Colin Toogood, the manager in charge of the Plymouth sorting office:

> It wasn't perceived as the individual's responsibility to immediately high-

light errors that were found as part of the old style of sampling. It was their responsibility to draw together a statistical picture of the office as a whole. The checker coming in from outside may well have thought that was the norm. The old style measurement didn't compare the data with anything that had gone on an hour before or an hour after. It was gathering information to get an overall quality picture.

If the inexperienced postman had continued sorting an hour a day for just four weeks without the error rate coming to light, it would have resulted in 5,000 mistakes – and a lot of customer complaints.

Treading carefully

The idea that postmen should check their own work was a revolutionary concept, however, and management at the Plymouth office knew they would have to tread carefully if the idea was to be taken up. The first step was to introduce some training. Says Williams, 'We thought if we just start putting control charts and sample forms all over the place, there won't be any understanding of it. There will be a bad reaction. So we took staff through a two hour awareness training programme of how to fill in the forms and what it was all about.'

Discussions during the training sessions raised the issue of what the Quality Diagnostics (QD) team, the traditional checkers, was going to do if the postmen sampled their own work. The postmen observed that in the past they had seen this team going around the floor of the sorting office with clip boards, but they did not really have a clue what they were doing. They also commented that in the past they only received negative feedback on their work. They were told about anything that went wrong, but they were never praised for excellent work. The postmen all agreed that they were the best people to do the checks since they were the people who had the most in-depth job knowledge of the work stations.

The postmen also took the opportunity to ask for additional work aids to make their sorting performance more efficient.

New relationship

The IPQM system has led to a new relationship between the postmen doing the sorting and the front-line managers, whose role is now that of coach. Garry Marshall used to be known as a supervisor at Plymouth, but is now called a front-line manager, a title more suited to his new role. He observes, 'Before the new measurement system was brought in supervisors were doing things like P40 checks. The men doing the sorting would always feel they were under the whip. Now they're doing their own checks they don't feel so threatened.'

Adds Toogood:

> It's certainly our intention to get to the position where the managers become leaders of the teams they are responsible for. My personal belief is that the only way forward is to lead the team rather than dictate every single move that the team makes. Devolution and empowerment are the key elements in that. Switching from supervisors to line-managers captures it all in the sense that we may well have changed the title, but the business still needs the support of people like Garry in being a manager and a leader. That comes from having the right culture within an office that encourages people to take on initiatives and not have to ask up the line whether it's OK.

Royal Mail management found that as soon as the postmen were consulted in the plans to switch to the IPQM system, all kinds of pent-up grievances and ill-feelings came out into the open. Notes Williams:

> Almost naturally there came out of it a lot of negative feelings about the existing measurements, which were all about kicking them up the back-side when things went wrong, about information they didn't understand because it was basically management information rather than information related to people's jobs.
>
> Then the feeling came out that the staff actually wanted to get involved.

The IPQM system met one of the most important criteria the post-men were seeking. That was the need for feedback on how well they were doing. The control charts provide them with instant information and wipe boards have been erected at strategic points around the Plymouth sorting office to record recurring mistakes to which the postmen should be alerted. This can, for example, draw their attention to the fact that there are two streets with the same name in the same locality. Says Keith Finch, a postman higher grade at Plymouth,

'The important thing is that although a mistake is identified, it's not identified to a person. It's a mistake that is common to everybody. It's an *aide memoire*, if you like. Something to jog your memory, so you don't forget what it is.'

Adds Toogood, 'There is no advantage to public ridicule. We just flag it up as a problem area, but the IPQM process allows us to bring a problem to an individual's attention and perhaps point to a training need.'

Another important development that has come from the introduction of IPQM are the fortnightly meetings between staff, management and the quality diagnostics team. They all come together to brainstorm for work improvement ideas.

Stumbling blocks

But the IPQM self-checking approach was not universally welcomed at Plymouth and some stumbling blocks initially stood in the way of implementation. Says Toogood:

> The first major issue we came across initially was time. Staff felt they didn't have time to do the sampling as well as the sorting. We considered that they did have time. The perception of how long it takes to sample twenty-five items every half hour is a lot more than it actually is.

It is simply a matter of flicking through a handful of letters and on many occasions there will be no wrongly sorted letters at all. It's all over in a matter of seconds. Adds Toogood:

> The reason we were determined it should be a member of staff and not someone from outside who did it was the question of ownership – ownership of the result and ownership of the responsibility for getting it right. I think that has been an extremely powerful message for the staff and ourselves.
>
> Possibly the only time there is a real problem is when we get very close to despatch time and we need to get through large volumes to make sure we get as much on the roads as we can. That can create some problems, but those problems have not been insurmountable.

The second important issue that came out of the exercise was the question of trust – trust on both sides. Says Toogood:

The cynical supervisors of old would have said you can't trust the devils to do an accurate count. What incentive have they got for actually recording the truth considering they are the ones who will look bad if the results are bad?

In fact, the trust needed to be developed on the part of the staff in considering that they were not going to be castigated if they did show that they had eight errors. In the case of the individual who did have eight errors in a sample, we undertook to give him training to demonstrate our commitment and support for the staff.

It might have been expected that the reaction of the quality diagnostics team would be negative, since the new system threatened to do away with their jobs. In fact, the QD team recognised that the new approach was helping to achieve higher levels of quality and enhanced their own efforts. They have been able to spend more time conducting in-depth analyses rather than wandering around the sorting office floor like the time-and-motion inspectors of old.

The reaction of the managers has been equally positive for the most part, although the enthusiasm has been greater among the youngest managers and those most recently promoted from the ranks. 'They realise that this is the sort of thing they'd have been looking for if they had still been postmen and they've been very supportive,' notes Toogood. 'It was important as far as I was concerned that this wasn't viewed as just another task. We wanted it to be viewed as something which will continue and therefore the message has been: "get involved now or get left behind".'

The IPQM system was introduced into two sorting areas in October 1992 and is steadily spreading to the rest of the office. Initial results have been highly encouraging. Errors have halved since its introduction. Cynics might suggest that this is the result of the sorters turning a blind eye to their own shortcomings. To avoid that criticism some downstream customer checks have been carried out which also indicate a fifty per cent improvement in the error rate.

Toogood cannot disguise his satisfaction at the way things are going. The Plymouth pilot project has been so successful that it is being introduced to other Royal Mail sorting offices in South Wales and the South West. 'The starting point,' he says, 'was the fact that I thought we needed to change the culture of the office from one where we supervise to one where we lead. We looked around for something that would allow us to achieve a number of goals – improve the quality of the job we do, give empowerment to the staff and change the culture of the office. We came up with the in-process quality measurement we have in place now.'

Product champions

The Plymouth sorting office has followed this up with other empowering ideas, such as creating 'product champions'. Postmen have been given specific responsibility to improve efficiency in certain work areas. For example, one of these product champions gives special attention to all mail destined for London. Another is dedicated to international mail. Says Toogood:

> One of these product champions is so enthusiastic about the idea he is holding training sessions and inviting experts to come and offer advice. We are letting him get on with it. We are giving him all the support we can and he's going at it hammer and tongs.
>
> The benefit, as I see it, is I've got a highly motivated postman who is dead keen to make the quality of his particular work area No. 1 in the country.

Toogood seems singularly unconcerned about whether product champions or any of the others empowered to take personal initiatives at the Plymouth sorting office will take their newfound freedom of action too far. 'I would say they should reach forward until they burn their fingers,' he insists. 'If we put obstacles in his way we shall never know how far an individual could take that particular area. I would rather the individual seek to improve the particular area they are responsible for as far as they can. Individuals tend to under-reach rather than over-reach. They will reach forward as far as they think they can; then they'll be looking over their shoulder and wondering if they can go a little bit further.'

Proud record

The IPQM system at Plymouth is helping to maintain – and hopefully improve – the Royal Mail's proud delivery record. Independent surveys show that ninety-four per cent of all first class mail is delivered the day following posting. A remarkable achievement when it is considered that it includes such remote areas as the Shetlands in the far north and The Scilly Isles in the far south west. It places the Royal Mail at the top of the league table in Europe and it is threatening to become No. 1 in the world.

Thoughts

Toogood indicated that major issues included trust and time. Managers and staff had to trust each other and the new way of working for it to make progress. If teams are to be empowered then trust is essential. Team members need to trust themselves and believe in their own competence, they need to trust each other – particularly when they are checking each other's work – and they need to trust their managers. If managers feel and act on the need to check up repeatedly then the team is likely to experience this as control and disempowering in its effect. Time was an issue for sorters in that they felt making quality checks might obstruct their ability to do their own jobs. That turned out not to be the case. More relevant in terms of time was the timeliness of the feedback. Instead of being given five days late it is provided almost instantaneously. Time is also an issue in the length of time it takes for changes to work through. The process of change in the sorting areas where IPQM was first introduced is not yet complete. The product champions are still pushing the change forward. Training was also an issue, training in IPQM and training in response to problems were important steps.

8

PREPARING THE GROUND (TRAINING)

A growing number of companies are sending managers on external courses, like those run by Ashridge Management College or Performance Consultants, to help them to make the often traumatic switch from a command and control style of management to becoming a coach.

Equally many companies are realising that the other side of the coin is that shopfloor workers and the front-line troops need to be trained to adjust to the increasing authority that is being devolved to them in the new climate of empowerment.

Although coaching itself is classic on-the-job training, preparation for coaching is conducted through more formal training. Training permits concentrated development over a short space of time with opportunities to practise, to receive feedback, to debate and discuss approaches to coaching, and to learn from others' experience.

At ICI's Merseyside operations a comprehensive training and career development programme has been devised for shopfloor workers which includes putting them through exercises that test their abilities to take on responsibilities that were previously regarded as the exclusive province of management. (This experience is detailed in the case study at the end of this chapter.)

Among the key aspects of the ICI experience is its focus on shopfloor workers, its determination not only to develop their skills but also to broaden their horizons and expand their self-perception in terms of their capabilities and their career opportunities. Using outdoor exercises, work-based projects involving cross-functional teams, individual assessments for development, educational support, wider selection searches for potential team leaders, and coaching courses for potential team leaders, ICI is determined that change goals determined from the top will be matched by a desire and capacity for change from the bottom.

In making such a large investment of time and resources in its shopfloor staff ICI is seeking to raise their capability to help ICI compete effectively. More specifically, the company has identified barriers to teamworking and competitiveness in old working practices. These difficulties were compounded by the organisational division of integrated tasks between separated individuals. A major part of the new programme is to raise people's awareness of the benefits of really effective teamworking, not just for ICI but in terms of broadening and deepening job skills. By linking these developments to extensive investments in its shopfloor staff, ICI is making clear its commitment to its staff and their development and its belief that such development is essential to maintain ICI's competitiveness.

This whole programme has also posed enormous challenges for ICI's first-line managers. Their commitment to coaching is exemplified by their involvement in the outdoor exercises where they are involved in providing feedback to participants. There are evidently coaching opportunities for all parties in this process. First-line managers who were promoted because of their expertise are wrestling with the issues of not intervening directly, of not becoming 'hands-on' even though that is what they are good at and enjoy. At the same time they are struggling with the need to delegate more of their work which is hard when it is that work which traditionally differentiated them from the shop floor.

Coaching rather than directing or taking over means that first-line managers have to ensure that the 'monkey' stays with the shopfloor. The development of the role of team leader below first-line management leaves team leaders in the ambiguous position of leading their equals while not relying on authority or being too directive. Given the changes in progress elsewhere, it is easy to see why the team leader's role is regarded as ideal training for first-level management.

ICI point to substantial cost savings and improvements in the quality of maintenance as a result of the programme. Perhaps even more impressive is the obvious enthusiasm and interest it has released among shopfloor workers. Such interest, enthusiasm and desire to grow are among the most valuable, if least tangible, outcomes of a shift to empowerment.

MORE DEMANDING TASKS

Similarly, Sainsbury's has introduced a number of programmes that help its front-line staff to extend their skills and take on more demanding tasks.

Sainsbury's was one of the sponsors of the *Employment in Britain* survey. Says Judith Evans, the company's director of corporate personnel, 'One of the issues to come out of the survey was how important careers are to people. It made us realise that if as an organisation we want to harness people's potential then we ought to be looking more seriously at what we are doing for careers. So we've introduced a programme called *Choices* which is targeted at the weekly paid staff and offers them career guidance.'

Personnel managers in forty of Sainsbury's branches have been given additional training in counselling to avoid the programme taking on a directive approach. Says Evans, 'It's very much employee-centred. The employee comes with an issue which may be that they want to move on in the organisation but they don't know how to do it. Another issue for people is that they want to contribute more in the jobs they've currently got, but they don't know how to go about it.'

Sainsbury's claims that ninety-six per cent of the employees who have been through the career guidance programme are clearer about where they want to go in the organisation and the training requirements to get there. It is supported by a programme called *Help Yourself to Education*, which offers employees sponsorship to undergo courses in their own time which are not directly related to performance on the job. Many employees are keen to improve their numeracy – a skill widely needed at all levels in a retail operation.

The programme is also aimed at people who lack confidence in expressing themselves in writing. 'I would say it's as much a question of confidence as it is ability,' suggests Evans.

A sixth of the 6,000 employees initially eligible have opted for Sainsbury's career guidance programme. Considering the group has around ten thousand part-time students working for it with little or no commitment to seeking a career with the organisation, this is a very gratifying response rate. So far the programme has only been piloted in three of of Sainsbury's twenty-seven districts, but all the participants are shopfloor workers who until now have never thought of going on a training course.

Says Evans:

> We have well-established career paths for people at management level. People with ability and commitment can move up quite easily. It is the opportunity of tapping into the weekly paid staff which is most unusual and where we felt we could do most good. The *Leadership through Teamwork* programme tackles it from the management point of view.
>
> We're working from both ends. We are asking managers to look at their coaching style and the extent to which they need to embody that in their activities (see Chapter Four) and also from the staff side to encourage them to come forward, but also to give them training and the skills they need to be able to contribute more.

DUE FINANCIAL PRUDENCE

In contrast to Sainsbury's and ICI Merseyside, Woolwich Building Society has focused on management development as the indirect means of developing its staff. The Woolwich, like other building societies, is conscious of the need to behave with due financial prudence and concern for its customers' interests. Historically, this encouraged the development of a bureaucratic command and control structure in such financial institutions. Procedures carefully prescribed how staff were to behave and what activity they were allowed to undertake. Limits of discretion were narrow.

Increasing competitive pressure encouraged a reconsideration of this approach at The Woolwich. Three objectives were set for a change programme: to improve business performance, to switch managers to a coaching style, and to clarify staff's role in relation to required standards and to indicate those areas where some individual initiative is possible and desirable.

The primary vehicle for this change has been the *Manager's Role in Learning* programme. Some 400 head office staff and branch managers have been through the programme. These managers have been trained to coach, educate and assess their staff so that they can identify and remedy performance issues and enable staff to clarify what is expected of them. A major part of this process has aimed at raising the confidence of front-line staff. Coaching is seen as a means of delivering flexibility in an otherwise prescriptive organisation, of enabling staff to test the boundaries of their discretion in those areas where this would not be contrary to policy. The Woolwich sees as one of its issues that not all of its staff want to test the boundaries. Some are keen to go on operating within the prescribed limits where they are more confident.

Using its middle managers to develop the front-line staff has, according to The Woolwich, been a considerable success. The impact on the business in handling enquiries and converting leads has been substantial.

UNITED

ICI Merseyside, Woolwich Building Society and Sainsbury's are united in their introduction of comprehensive training programmes, in which coaching plays a key role. ICI and Sainsbury's have both sought to support the change in management style and its impact on business performance by directly involving their work forces in personal development and career widening initiatives. The Woolwich has initially concentrated more heavily on its line managers and involved them in the process of developing front-line staff. Raising the confidence and broadening the horizons of front-line staff is a key element in all three organisations' approaches.

All three have similar goals of changing managerial style, developing front-line staff and improving business performance. They have chosen different route maps. All are facing major hurdles in terms of changing not only management style but organisational culture to shift the expectations, values and behaviours of staff throughout the organisation. All are reporting substantial success in meeting all of their objectives. It appears that coaching can take many forms and still be successful.

Case study

ICI MERSEYSIDE

The Merseyside operations of ICI Chemicals and Polymers at Runcorn in Cheshire was formed some six years ago with the merging of a number of separate sites, each of which had their own culture, hierarchy and management style. In trying to forge these disparate elements into one harmonious organisation it was resolved to focus strongly on providing training and development opportunities for all of the 2,600 employees. Says Peter Hyam, engineering manager, North West Operations, 'Our philosophy is one of giving everybody the opportunity to have a career rather than a job and a career implies development and individuals gaining in self-confidence and feeling capable of taking initiatives.'

To achieve this, ICI Merseyside has put together a complete programme that is not just addressed to one part of the working population, but which offers a career path and training tracks from entry point up to management. The programme is a mixture of a bottom-up and a top-down approach with the full commitment of senior management.

ICI has not entrusted this comprehensive training and development programme to a separate functional organisation. It firmly believes that training and development is a line responsibility. Says Hyam:

> We have a strong belief in Merseyside operations that training, development, recruitment and career progression of people is very much a line management activity. I see that as one of the most important parts of my job and the most important part of the jobs of all the people who work with me. We are not in the business of leaving training and development to a personnel or training department.

The career progression programme was launched in the central maintenance department, which represents about half of the total Merseyside maintenance work force, but has since spread to the operations side of the business. Weekly staff are offered a career path and training track tailored to their needs which will eventually take some of them into management.

Outward bound

One of the initial personal development activities offered to all weekly paid staff is an outward bound course, which is run in North Yorkshire by an outside training organisation about twelve times a year. Around 600 people have already been through it. The intention is that all 1,600 weekly staff employees will eventually participate. Says Joanna Cooper, head of central maintenance at ICI Merseyside, 'The outward bound course focuses very much on teamworking and teamworking skills – traditional areas of communication and working together – but it also starts to introduce concepts of what makes a good leader and actually gives people the opportunity to try that out.'

Although the specific exercises, such as building a raft within a fixed time frame, are designed by the outside training organisation, the participants – twenty on each course – are coached by ICI's own first-line managers, which provides them with a training ground to practise their own skills.

Cooper sees the outward bound activities as a way to start to generate confidence in the hourly paid workers that they can handle activities outside the confines of their technical skills. This prepares the ground for them to be able to take on greater responsibilities in the work environment, a prerequisite for a coaching style of management that requires managers to stand back and take a less authoritarian role in running their operations. Says Cooper:

> All of a sudden you see very visibly the realisation in some of the individuals that they can actually take on quite a lot, that they can achieve quite a lot. Maybe they're actually quite good as a leader or they can actually get up and make a presentation, stand up in front of a group and speak. You actually see the change within a week. It's quite dramatic.

Hyam points out that participants on the outward bound course also get their first taste of such management skills as planning and organising:

> In the first one or two exercises they make an absolute mess of things and fall flat on their face. They then have to face up to the fact that if you stop and think and understand the objective and make a simple plan that you follow, life becomes considerably easier. People's natural tendency,

certainly in the kind of operations we are in, is, given a problem, they jump in with both feet, have the adrenalin flowing and work like stink, but often go round in circles.

The first-line managers who act as coaches on the outward bound courses, and who will themselves have been through the course at an earlier stage, are there to provide feedback after observing the participants in action. Says Hyam:

Sometimes the feedback is not the most flattering for the individual, but we see a big benefit coming out of it. It can be simple things like: 'You don't listen' or 'you talk non-stop and you put down others who have good ideas'. The coaches are also participants. They can't just stand aside and give people instructions.

Shortly after returning to work, the outward bound course participants give a presentation to management about what they have learned and how it translates back to their work environment. According to Hyam this tends to generate in every case 'very productive, open discussions'.

Link back

This is followed up by what is called a link-back-to-work project, in which weekly paid staff are put to the test as to whether they have really picked up new skills that make them more independent in the work place. A team is formed and a team leader is appointed and they are given a free hand to tackle a project that requires the kind of concentration of skills normally associated with management.

The projects are far from paper exercises. One, for example, required a team of weekly paid staff to build a training rig. They were given a set of line drawings and the rest was up to them. The training rig they were expected to build was a full-size model of a process plant used by maintenance workers and operators to learn and practise skills. It is like a mini-chemical plant with a tank, pump, valves and instruments and a control room to operate the equipment remotely. The only difference was that for safety reasons, water was used to flow through the rig rather than chemicals. Says Cooper:

The individuals that were in that group are members of the shopfloor so they are actually used to being given a tremendous amount of direction in terms of setting up a project – the foreman saying: 'can you go and remove or replace those pieces of equipment' not 'can you build that?' I briefed one individual as team leader who had to go away and think about the team members he needed to do the project. I then briefed the team.

Cooper asked the team to estimate how much time they would want to prepare a budget and a draft plan for building the rig. Once they had decided on that, they went back to Cooper and made a presentation. At that point she decided whether or not to let them go ahead. 'There was no involvement at all from management – first-line managers, supervisors or anybody,' insists Cooper. 'I briefed the individuals directly and they came back to me with their plans and went ahead and did it. It proved that they had organisational skills, not just technical skills.'

The shopfloor workers could hardly believe their own abilities. Recalls Cooper:

When they were first briefed on the project there were looks of shock on their faces at the extent to which they were actually being asked to get involved. There are always people there to help them but it had to be at their request. They had some ups and downs on the project. It didn't go exactly to plan and that was part of the learning for them. But what they achieved was absolutely outstanding.

They made such a good job of the project that the training rig is now in regular use at ICI.

Barriers in the mind

One of the real advantages of the link-back exercise is that it is performed by a cross-functional team that has been taken out of the operating environment and given the opportunity to work together in a completely new set of circumstances. The team members are not bound by former entrenched operating practices. Says Cooper:

If you look at the normal jobs, the individual may well be a fitter or an electrician or a process operator, so their role is quite clearly defined within the prescribed boundaries which exist culturally within their organisation. Here there were no boundaries opposite which they had to work. They were all removed from that. They were deliberately off-site so that they were not immediately rubbing up against work issues. The only boundaries that existed were the barriers in their minds and they had some difficulties with some of that.

For example, they had some discomfort about how far they could go in ignoring demarcation issues. Of course if the manager is saying 'I don't care how far you go', that actually gives them some difficulty as well, because they actually want you to tell them, because that's what they're used to.

'Total amazement'

John Williams, who has been a process operator at ICI since 1979, describes his reaction as one of 'total amazement' when confronted with the training rig exercise. 'There were eight lads plucked from all these different courses thrown together with a set of blueprints and told "Build that and we will come back in eight weeks and see how you got on." It was absolutely wonderful.'

The outward bound course stood Williams in good stead. 'If I hadn't been on that I would probably have stood back and watched everybody else, but there is something about that course that gives you confidence and convinces you that you can do things as well as anybody else.'

The team Williams worked with ran into a real snag when they found that there was a drain running underneath where they planned to build the rig and had to start all over again. 'I don't know if they planned it that way; there was one obstacle after another for us to overcome. It was very much the real world.'

The training rig exercise also gave the shopfloor workers a taste of some of the problems managers have to confront. From time to time, the team of eight needed to draft in extra hands to help out and experienced some difficulty in managing these additional people. For example, some of them went on holiday part way through the exercise, leaving the team in the lurch, which was something of a shock to them. Says Cooper:

They were faced with a lot of the issues their managers are faced with.

There was also a realisation and understanding of why maybe when they went on to a particular job not everything was actually there, but it also, very importantly, gave them some of the abilities and the understanding about how they could tackle that problem rather than to sit back and think it's not my job. All of a sudden, we're equipping them with some of the skills to actually do something about the problem.

Community work

Some of the link-back projects involve community work. One team refurbished a local community centre, for example. Another converted a domestic science classroom at a local college to make it accessible to disabled children. In all these projects the team of shopfloor workers procures the necessary materials based on the plans supplied and then manages the execution of the project from start to finish, working to a predetermined budget. The community projects have an added bonus, as Hyam points out:

> They do us a lot of good in terms of PR. They do the individuals a tremendous amount of good because they're putting into practice things they have learned; they're directly interfacing with the customer who is sometimes a vicar, sometimes a person from the local authority, sometimes the headmaster of a school. All the reports we've had back have been extremely encouraging.

After each project the team makes a presentation to Hyam and Cooper outlining how well they believe they have met the remit they were set. This leads to a general discussion about the advantages of working as a multi-functional team. A common comment is that the exercise was free of the sort of demarcation issues that arise in the normal work environment. Says Hyam:

> Of course that allows us then to be more provocative and say 'If it was that satisfying converting a class for the use of disabled children in Widnes, why can't we have the environment where we have the same satisfaction for you here at work?' All of this is building up to translating from the event to the linking-back to that culture beginning to be the norm in the work place and we can see a lot of that's beginning to happen.

Union co-operation

Although ICI Merseyside is blunt about its aim to reduce demarcation disputes because they stand in the way of the kind of team spirit that it is trying to generate, Hyam does not foresee any problems with the unions:

> People make a lot of fuss about the unions. The unions are there to fill management incompetence and the management vacuum. We neither think we're incompetent nor do we have a vacuum and all our weekly staff are in effect union members and all our shop stewards are employees. They all go through the outward bound course and the linking-back-to-work exercise as individuals. In some cases the shop stewards actually get chosen as the leader for the linking-back-to-work exercise; in some cases they aren't. They all mix in exactly like everyone else.
>
> Our whole objective is to get people to behave as people naturally wish to behave. People aren't born indolent and demarcated; we make them that way and I think this is a very important message to get across – what we're doing here is trying to remove all the constraints which in many cases management have imposed. Demarcations are a management problem, nobody else's, and it's usually management that makes people indolent because we force people to wait for something; we're not properly organised.

Escaping the strait-jacket

John Williams revels in the change of culture at ICI that has 'taken the strait-jacket' off shopfloor workers. 'When I first started at ICI everyone was pigeon-holed. Once a process operator, always a process operator. It was only a question of what would go first – your hair or your motivation. That's all changed now.'

Adds Williams, who enjoys water ski-ing and power boat racing in his spare time, 'Everything I found interesting up to a couple of years ago was outside of work. Now the amazing thing is I find I'm enjoying myself inside work. It's amazing how much you get involved.'

Explicit

ICI is very explicit in what it tells the shopfloor workers it expects them to get out of the career development programme. It tells them that they are being put through a development programme that is no different in effect to what has traditionally been done for graduates and management in order to equip them with a career rather than a job and to help them understand the importance of teamwork. 'We want them to feel they are working in an environment that is open and free and where everybody has a contribution to make and where initiatives are welcomed. There's no disguising what we are doing,' stresses Hyam.

Cooper and Hyam are often asked why ICI is spending so much money to develop shopfloor workers. The answer, says Hyam, 'is that in the end we want to remain a highly competitive business that is going to guarantee jobs for the future. This for us is the most important part of getting more effective, more efficient, beating the competition, so that all of us here have jobs in the future.'

Effective teamworking is seen at ICI Merseyside as the best way to achieve efficiency and secure survival into the future with management playing more of a coaching and supporting role. Says Hyam:

> All of us in one way or another work in teams. The problem in the past is that teamworking has had to operate despite the setting up of demarcated jobs by management. If you take for example the renewing of a piece of equipment, it means having to shut down the plant, which is one person's job; then the new equipment has to be got from the stores; that's somebody else's job. There are delays and frustrations at each of those interfaces.
>
> If you actually put a team together that sees the whole task as being something it's accountable for and needs to do, all those interfaces disappear. They all help each other and it's not necessarily the man who did it last time whose job it is to go to stores.
>
> If you have a team that is working effectively, that first of all understands its objective and knows the time and budget constraints it is operating under and is properly constituted with the right blend of skills, why on earth do you need somebody else telling them what to do when they are clear about what to do themselves?

No more sitting around

What ICI is trying to get away from is the idea that the shopfloor supervisor is there to solve all the minor problems that arise during a piece of routine work. In the past this has meant that shopfloor workers have been sitting around idle while the supervisor goes off to tackle whatever minor setback has brought work to a halt. A classical example is the maintenance worker who can't get on with the job because he has been given the wrong gasket. He goes to the supervisor and tells him that he has the wrong gasket and expects the supervisor to sort it out while he sits and waits, doing nothing. In the new situation the maintenance worker probably tells the supervisor that he has the wrong piece of equipment, but goes himself to stores to get the right gasket and goes back to the job and gets on with it. 'That makes an enormous difference,' insists Hyam.

Says Cooper:

> What we are trying to do is to get the individuals to solve the problems themselves and move the task along. That's what we're equipping them to do by showing them ways of working together. We want the individuals to have the ability and the confidence to tackle problems themselves, so that what the supervisor is doing is coaching them to do that, so that when an individual presents that supervisor with a problem the response of the supervisor is not: 'I'll take that problem away from you', but 'how can I help you to solve it?'

For John Williams, taking on responsibilities he would never have contemplated in the past has been highly motivating. For example, he was put in charge of a £50,000 overhaul, which involved shutting down a plant at ICI Merseyside. 'My job used to be walking around taking readings and monitoring things; other people used to do the rest of the work. But I ran that project with a team of boiler workers and one other process guy to help me. I coordinated it and ran it as opposed to just being the process guy, which is something that had never happened to me before.'

Changing titles

ICI plans to emphasise this change of approach by doing away with the title of supervisor and replacing it with first-line manager, whose responsibilities will be very clearly spelled out. Explains Hyam:

The first-line manager's job, first and foremost, is to be very clear about the task that needs to be done, so that he can communicate that. Secondly, he's responsible for picking the appropriate team. Thirdly, he equips them with the freedom and the skills to be able to do that. Fourthly, he is available when there is really a problem or some decision on priority that the team either would not be allowed to make in a certain set of circumstances or that the team has not got the confidence to make. But he is no longer the expert in that particular trade discipline.

Some time after taking part in the outward bound course, ICI shopfloor workers have the opportunity to attend a course called *Developing for the Future*. This is a three day course, which concentrates on the individual as opposed to the teamworking aspects of the outward bound event. Individuals undergo a number of exercises that help them to identify their strengths and weaknesses and the direction they would like to see their careers going in. They leave the course with an action plan to help them realise their career aspirations.

Selection events

In the second phase of its development programme for shopfloor workers, ICI Merseyside runs a whole series of selection events that attempt to identify the people with the potential to move up the organisation to become first-line managers. As part of this programme selected individuals are sent on the coaching course based on sports coaching concepts run by Performance Consultants at the Lillishall National Sports Centre (see Chapter Four).

ICI Merseyside is unusual in that it sends hourly paid workers on a course that is generally seen as an exercise for management. It sees the course as particularly relevant for team leaders. Says Cooper:

Team leaders are potentially in quite a difficult situation because they're not really recognised as a line manager. They're a member of a team but they're still expected to take on a leadership role. So the skills that are picked up on the coaching course are readily usable and in some ways more readily usable by the team leaders than they are by first-line managers.

For Ernie Ratcliffe, a supervisor at ICI Merseyside, the sports coaching course made a lot of sense. He has been involved in team sports since the age of ten and currently coaches a local football team. Coaching has been his 'life style' and he is certain that it has rubbed off at work. However, he contends that the 'telling mode' of coaching is sometimes necessary both in sport and at work. He argues that the half-time pep talk can work wonders to re-invigorate a flagging football team.

Ratcliffe acknowledges, however, that at work the style of the supervisor has changed radically. 'The supervisor was God, but over the past twenty years, especially the last five or ten years, that isn't so.'

The hardest part for the supervisor, Ratcliffe admits, is to stand back and let his team get on with the work. 'But if you've developed people to the standard they need to be at, it's a lot easier to delegate. But you don't let go the reins. You've still got to keep your fingers on them so you can pull them back in again.'

A mechanical engineer by training, Ratcliffe often finds himself responsible for teams of technicians with skills he is less familiar with, which leaves him little option but to play the role of the coach. 'I expect the individual to be able to solve eighty-five to ninety per cent of any problems that arises because we train and develop them.'

Simon Maw, a mechanical lead tradesman at ICI Merseyside, has found that supervisors are less involved in day-to-day operations because they themselves are having greater responsibilities delegated to them.

> My supervisor has other roles now. He delegates things down to me because he's had things delegated down to him. Many of the supervisors have now become mini-accountants and mini-personnel departments all rolled into one. Therefore they spend less time on the job and more time in an office somewhere. The things they aren't doing on the job I pick up.
>
> I think some supervisors find it hard to delegate because they've been brought up in a culture that doesn't allow them to let go of responsibilities. They feel the need to keep an eye on everything because they're working in a dangerous industry.

For Maw the main problem has been having to give instructions as a team leader to fellow shopfloor workers whom he has worked with on an equal basis for a number of years. He admits that it filled him with apprehension. He picked up some useful tips on the sports coaching course, however, that have helped him overcome the difficulty. He has learned to build a rapport with his team members by talking with them about their outside interests rather than focusing on work issues all the time.

Logical progression

The structure of ICI Merseyside's development programme for shopfloor workers follows a very logical progression. It starts with learning about teamwork, planning and problem solving and gaining confidence in personal abilities. Following on from that, the participants study their personal strengths and weaknesses and set themselves on a career path. Then, for those who make the grade, there comes coaching skills to equip them to become team leaders and subsequently a first-line manager.

Sums up Hyam, 'In time everybody in every role will have had the training, the development and the experience to enable them to fulfil that role to the full.'

Hyam estimates that the shopfloor career development programme has cost in the region of £800,000 over a three year period. 'If you ask me whether we've had a return on that I would think that all the indications are that we've had that back twice over in terms of greater efficiency in the work place.'

One measure of this is the fact that ICI is using fewer people than before on routine maintenance work and there is much less lost time from recurring breakdowns. 'Another measure,' says Hyam 'is how many leaks do we have when we try to recommission a plant compared with previously. We have a tenth now of what we used to have. Why? Because people are better motivated; they now see it as their pride whereas in the past if it leaked it was somebody else's job to put it right.'

But the real measure is the high degree of enthusiasm among the shopfloor workers who are finding all kinds of new avenues opening up for them. John Williams has been spreading his own 'born again' enthusiasm among his fellow shopfloor workers with such missionary zeal that he found a Jehovah's Witness sticker inside his locker door. Such light-hearted humour doesn't bother him. He is too busy making plans to broaden his career. In fact, he has become so smitten by the company courses he has participated in that he has successfully applied to become a trainer himself.

WOOLWICH BUILDING SOCIETY

Woolwich Building Society is the third largest in the UK with more than 550 branches and 600 agencies. It has assets of over £20 billion, with more than 2.5 million investors and approximately half a million borrowers buying their own homes with the society's help.

A training needs analysis in 1991 resulted in The Woolwich introducing a major programme that involves teaching around 400 branch and head office managers to coach their staff to gain the confidence and competence to take on broader responsibilities. The programme, called the Managers' Role in Learning (MRL), won the Employment Department's National Training Award in 1992.

Apart from improving managers' coaching techniques and helping staff to reach the higher level of competence needed in an empowered organisation, the programme has led to significant advances in business performance. There has been a substantial increase in the number of business referrals from counter staff that have been converted into sales and improved interviewing techniques have also led to an upsurge in business.

The programme has been developed as a result of The Woolwich's concern that empowerment can only work if the front-line staff have the confidence to attain the kind of working standards that are required in a financial services organisation. Because of the nature of the business, there are many prescribed work procedures that have to be adhered to, but outside these there are 'grey areas' in which staff can be given the opportunity to show personal initiative.

Top management felt that it was necessary both to ensure that staff were fully competent at achieving the prescribed aspects of their job and that branch managers had the ability to assess this competence and to coach staff in testing the boundaries and exploring the grey areas that could lead to greater autonomy of action.

Payoffs

Improvements in coaching, training, assessment and feedback as a result of the programme have led to some significant payoffs for The Woolwich:

- Increases in referral rates from counter staff of up to 120 per cent
- Increases in conversion rates by interview staff of up to fifty per cent
- Greater ownership of some processes by staff, as managers involve them more via coaching, resulting in reduced time to complete procedures
- Greater understanding of staff needs and motivation, leading to higher levels of commitment throughout the branches
- Greater commitment to teamwork as a result of increased openness and support at all levels of the organisation.

One of the building society's regions has reported increased sales of around £74,000 as a direct result of improvements in referrals, within months of introducing coaching.

Values

In 1991 The Woolwich formulated ten value statements to epitomise what it wanted to achieve as an organisation. One of the value statements concerned the need to delegate decision making to the point closest to the customer. Another value statement involved training staff to draw out their full potential. Says David Beckett, the society's training and development manager, 'Taking those two values, coaching and the responsibility of the manager and the individual for their own development is something we are constantly trying to bring to the fore and trying to shift the balance of decision making away from central areas to the line.'

Like many organisations, The Woolwich recognises that empowerment is a desirable aim, but it is cautious about the kind of decisions it can leave to the discretion of its staff. If it allows too much autonomy it could lead to an inconsistency of service throughout its network of branches. Adhering to prescribed procedures is a way of ensuring this consistency. Says Beckett:

> We've learned from experience you need to define where your boundaries are. We are now going through a process of defining those

boundaries and clarifying the realms in which empowerment can operate. We need to operate within boundaries which say total empowerment leads to chaos but avoiding a totally controlled environment in which nobody dares make any decisions. We are working towards a model that says these are the parameters within which to operate. If you go beyond those parameters there needs to be an assessment of risk.

As far as The Woolwich is concerned the first step to empowerment is ensuring that staff are clear about what their work role is. Once this is clarified, staff can begin to explore the boundaries and identify the areas where they can operate at their own discretion. Says Beckett:

> Any financial institution has quite big responsibilities in terms of rules and regulations and those policies need to be interpreted. We are working on a process at the moment for the underwriting sector which defines the factors that need to be taken into consideration and where the grey areas are.

For example, when the society is considering lending money to a customer, checking references is an important part of the decision making. 'You have a certain amount of discretion in your decision making, but it needs to be informed,' points out Beckett. 'In the same way, in terms of offering financial advice, we are very prescriptive in the sense that the financial advice must be beneficial to the customer and must follow a particular pattern in terms of how to manage the interview. That is because we are regulated in that sort of framework and because it delivers a benefit.'

Beckett argues that if staff understand the standards they are expected to operate to, it is much easier to provide feedback on how well they are performing. But he recognises that there is a danger that if those standards are too prescriptive staff will feel constrained and unlikely to contribute ideas for working more effectively.

> This is why exploring the boundaries becomes important. In under-writing, for example, we have clear operating boundaries. It is the exploration of the grey areas that is increasingly important in the coaching process. The organisational approach is quite prescriptive. The coaching approach isn't, because it is wedded to the individual. If the individual has an issue or a goal he or she wishes to achieve we work with that.

Testing the boundaries

Coaching, in Beckett's view, is a way of allowing staff to test the boundaries at their own pace and in their own time. It provides the opportunity for them to clarify their current position and examine whether they would like to expand their present work load. 'It may make sense to stay where you are, because, from what we've discovered from going through this coaching process, an individual may not have got to the point which enables him or her to make decisions they feel comfortable with, let alone decisions the manager feels comfortable with.'

The prescribed working patterns The Woolwich is obliged to lay down in many aspects of its operations are not as confining as they may seem at first sight since the staff are involved in establishing the standards in the first place. They are asked whether the standards make sense to them and whether they are the kind of policies they can work with and indeed, whether they need to be changed. Says Beckett:

> It's a question of getting the involvement right and also explaining there has been involvement is very important, because, given that we have 550 branches nationwide, you can't involve every branch and every region. Even if you had a process of saying 'we wish to involve, we wish to empower, we wish you to improve the process', at the end of the day the process has to be consistent from one branch to another. But you have got to have the organisational capability to go beyond those boundaries and to develop the ability of assessing the risk of doing that, because there is a risk. Certainly in underwriting there is a risk of making a bad judgement and that can be very costly. You need something like a rock of certainty before you start exploring the boundaries.
>
> I feel very strongly about having a core of activities, an anchor that people can be wedded to before they start to spread into other areas. In a sense, they have the security of going back and saying: 'at least I'm doing what is expected of me.' Or 'if I'm going beyond that, I know why I'm going beyond that'.

The Woolwich has gone through the process of establishing the standards in key operating areas such as underwriting and customer interviewing and has begun the process, through coaching, of exploring how its staff can go beyond the boundaries set by these standards. The starting point was that it was necessary for managers to have the capability of supporting staff throughout the exploratory phase. 'We have put most of our energy into training our managers, certainly throughout the retail network, in the skills of how to coach, train and develop the individual,' says Beckett.

Improving business performance

The focal point of the coaching has been improving business performance. This has meant that The Woolwich has been able to achieve three prime aims. It has helped its managers to switch to the coaching style of management that is a prerequisite for introducing empowerment in any organisation. The staff have been helped to clarify their role in the organisation, both in terms of the standards they are expected to achieve and the areas where they can push forward the boundaries. At the same time the end goal has been to improve business performance, quality and productivity.

This three-pronged approach has produced some significant benefits. Switching to the coaching style of management is not an easy transition for most managers after years of operating in a command and control mode. If, however, they can, through coaching, see evidence of their staff coming to grips with the competencies necessary to fulfil a more empowered role, they will be less nervous about taking the risks involved. The staff, for their part, will feel more inclined to take personal initiatives if they are confident about their capability to perform their core work and – just as importantly – they feel confident that their manager recognises their abilities. This confidence is reinforced if the changed way of operating produces significant improvements in work performance, as has been the case at The Woolwich. Says Beckett:

> There are a number of transitions that need to be worked through. The first one is that we are adopting a very structured approach in terms of 'these are the standards and this is what you need to do in order to achieve the standards', which at first sight is quite threatening for people to go through. It's saying we are going to make sure you can actually do it.
>
> Traditionally, most human resource work and training seems to have

been on the basis that you attend a programme, you go away and we assume you can actually do it. So we are talking about a significant switch in operation. We are not going to assume; we are going to have measures which may be behaviour observations, sampling of the change afterwards; we'll check.

I think once people recognise after being observed that they can actually achieve what is expected of them, they can start to push back the boundaries. It adds clarity to the process. People know what they're being judged against. The first concern is almost the opposite of empowerment, because it's seen as inspection, but once you get beyond that you can take it further, which is where the coaching process comes in.

Coaching skills

Looking for a way to train its branch managers in coaching skills, Beckett came across Performance Consultants, the training organisation run by three former international sports coaches. Beckett decided to put his own management team through the programme run by Performance Consultants, which uses sporting analogies to put across its theories.

Based on that experience, Beckett devised a tailor-made training model together with Performance Consultants for use in-house. This aimed at giving branch managers the skills not only of a coach but of an educator in the work place and of an assessor of competence. The idea was that assessing competence would reveal the shortfalls in ability and indicate the areas on which to focus the coaching.

An in-house pilot programme was produced. Before attending the training session, branch managers were given a video explaining the GROW coaching model advocated by Performance Consultants (see Chapter Four). This included interviews with Woolwich managers who had already been through the course, explaining how it had benefited them personally. In this way, course members were able to familiarise themselves with the sporting analogies prior to the actual training and could see that lessons from sport could have some relevance to a building society manager.

By the end of 1992 some 400 managers had been through the coaching programme, which again focused on the two key areas of counter staff referrals and interviewing techniques. The view was that the benefits of the programme would be far easier to measure if it was built around improving specific areas of business performance than if it was purely an academic exercise. This indeed proved to be the case. 'There was something like £70,000 additional revenues being earned per programme when we measured the results afterwards through increased referrals and increased business from interviews,' says Beckett with some satisfaction.

> My guess is, if it runs to the same form as other programmes, that there will be a tail-off, because what we've discovered from measuring over a three month period is that after reaching a peak there is a tail-off. Normally it doesn't go back to previous levels, but it doesn't carry on at the peak levels.
>
> The anecdotal feedback from the managers is that they felt more comfortable in terms of being with staff and running through perform-ance problems and that improved results were coming through.

The Woolwich has found that the feedback its managers can provide during the coaching process is particularly useful for obtaining improved performances. Says Beckett:

> The manager can assess how the individuals are doing, rate them and give them feedback. When we've actually trained people and measured their business performance afterwards there has been a step change in their performance. If people have that degree of clarity there is a clear business improvement. Certainly we have seen it in the commission earnings of our financial advisers.'

Realistic

Beckett is frank about the number of Woolwich managers who are likely to embrace wholeheartedly the coaching approach to training.

> I would guess about fifty per cent of them would claim they are probably doing it; the other fifty per cent would claim they're doing it or are considering doing it, but some of them really aren't. I would say that's quite a success, given that it's our first go at it.
>
> For some managers, making the switch has been very difficult. A lot of it is to do with attitude of mind. It's going back to Theory X and Theory Y (the theories of authoritarian versus participative management styles of

US behavioural scientist Douglas McGregor). If you're a Theory X manager this is totally unacceptable. If you're Theory Y, it's 'Thank you very much; I like that; give me some more.' It depends on where you think the average British manager sits.

In Beckett's experience, coaching comes more naturally to sales managers who are accustomed to passing on their experience to less experienced salesmen. Administrative managers embrace coaching with less enthusiasm in general because they tend to have grown up in a command and control ethos. 'Administration tends to be set up with stable systems. Selling is all about fluidity and movement, although it's not always that clear cut.'

Nor is Beckett totally convinced that the Woolwich managers are coaching precisely to the model suggested by Performance Consultants. They are more likely, in his view, to develop an approach they feel comfortable with personally. 'The value of a model is that it gives a route map. Whether you use that route map is not really important provided you get to the same end point of getting the individual to own the problem and move towards resolution for themselves and feel that to be a personal responsibility.'

The next phase for The Woolwich, having put its middle management ranks through the coaching course, is to provide the same experience for its senior executives. There were plans to introduce a senior management course in the autumn of 1993. This was to be followed by a feedback programme in which the staff being coached by senior management will be questioned about the impact they feel it has on their work performance.

THE CHARACTERISTICS OF THE MANAGEMENT COACH

To mis-quote Shakespeare, all the world is a team and one coach in her time plays many parts.

Managers often resist switching to a coaching style because they are reluctant to exchange the familiar for the unknown. They suspect they are giving up the tangible command and control mode of operating for something that is far more esoteric, even though coaching has been around as long as mankind has organised itself into teams for work or recreation or entertainment. In fact, the role of the coach is multi-faceted and embraces a far broader range of skills and talents than those practised by the single-purpose autocrat.

In coaching there are at least three levels the manager has to work at: the organisational/environmental level, the team level and the individual level. Each of these places different demands on the coach, which are met by filling different roles, but there is an underlying similarity of skills required in all these roles.

The guide

Beginning at the individual level of one-to-one coaching, each stage of the CALAIS loop requires the coach to fulfil a different role (Fig. 9.1). In the *Criteria Setting* stage the coach acts as a guide, helping the trainee to identify the various interested parties whose needs must be considered in relation to the action – customers, end users, colleagues – and to understand the criteria by which they and the trainee will judge her success. These criteria will include learning targets and, as we saw in The Woolwich case study in Chapter Eight, business performance targets. A trainee accustomed to simply being told what to do will begin by being unaware of these other dimensions. The role of the guide is not to tell the trainee who the interested parties are or what their criteria will be, but to help her draw them out for herself. In the Sainsbury's 'Bruised Apples' case in Chapter Six the intervening manager might well ask 'How would you feel as a customer if you bought bruised fruit?' and use this to draw out new criteria for performance. The guide also needs to help the trainee to rate her own performance and identify those areas she wishes to improve at this stage. Again, the emphasis in the CALAIS loop is on enabling the trainee to see these issues for herself rather than imposing them.

The consultant

In the *Awareness Building* phase of the loop, the coach acts as a consultant. This role is much tougher than that of simply pointing out the performance issues to the trainee, although many managers find even that profoundly uncomfortable. As a consultant, the coach is helping the trainee identify appropriate sources of feedback and understand the meaning of that feedback. This includes encouraging the trainee to acknowledge feedback she has already received – positive and negative – and appreciate its significance. Until the trainee has a clearer appreciation of her current performance, she is likely to lack the knowledge and incentive to change. The aim of the consultant in this phase is to develop the trainee to the point where she can manage her own awareness building without assistance from the consultant. The consultant role is not just about being warm and friendly, although that may, on occasion, be appropriate. It demands integrity of the highest order, combined with sensitivity and tact. Colluding with the trainee to ignore or deny uncomfortable pieces of feedback is to short change her and inhibit her scope for development. Timing is important in this process but 'never' is not within the acceptable time frames.

The intellectual challenger

If the consultant role demands integrity, the intellectual challenger role in the *Logical Analysis* phase requires intellectual strength and commitment, a willingness to challenge and discuss to enable the trainee to understand the causes as well as the effects of current performance levels. Perhaps because our concept of coaching is so influenced by sporting analogies we tend to neglect the analysis of cause and effect. But even in sport, if a hockey player persistently finds herself out of position it is inadequate to tell her what to do without understanding what it is she is trying to do and why she is trying to do it.

In relation to business issues, the coach as intellectual challenger is encouraging people to reconsider familiar thought patterns and go beyond them, to refuse to settle for the known and to try for the unknown. When Capp told the outage team at Hartlepool that he wanted it completed in twelve not sixteen weeks he was simultaneously setting criteria in a directive manner and intellectually challenging in a coaching manner. When the team went to consider other power stations and other organisations they were intellectually challenging themselves by acknowledging that things could be done differently and that different might be better.

The encourager/creator

The *Alternatives Generation and Evaluation* phase was one where the difference between the expert and helper models of coaching was most marked. In the expert model the coach would indicate the way forward on the basis of her experience and expertise. If there is an acknowledged 'best way', the expert coach would see this as the appropriate route. In the CALAIS loop, the coach seeks to enable the trainee to invent a range of alternatives and evaluate them. The primary role for the coach here is that of encouraging and providing space. At ICI Merseyside, managers deliberately stepped back from the project teams to give team members the experience of inventing solutions for themselves. The excitement and interest that generated was palpable.

If the trainee is stuck, the coach may draw on her experience or her creativity to suggest tentatively another idea which could be examined. At issue here is the creation of ownership. If the trainee can devise her own solution to the issue, she is more likely to use and to develop it than if it is imposed. By creating 'product champions' in the Royal Mail sorting offices in Plymouth, management unlocked a stream of creativity to which previously they had had no access. The impact on trainee confidence of successfully solving problems for themselves is enormous.

The virtual coach

In virtual reality, electronics are used to simulate reality to the extent that people react as if it were reality. In the *Implementation* phase the coach aims not to be there at all while having created such a strong sense of reality in the earlier phases that the trainee can coach herself. The temptation for managers at this point to intervene, to assist, to lend a hand is very strong, perhaps because that is the old style they are comfortable with or perhaps because they are genuinely interested in the task. Either way the temptation must be resisted. Coaches who continue to shout instructions while the game is in progress are revealing a lack of confidence in the trainees and ultimately in themselves. If awareness building is to be internalised then it is important at the implementation phase to allow the trainee to concentrate on what she is doing. Shouts from the sidelines are a distraction. This approach does not prevent the coach standing on the sidelines and monitoring progress. Such information will be needed later in the loop. Nor does it deny the right to answer if asked for assistance, although the helper coach is more likely to answer a question with a question as she continues to develop the trainee.

The mirror

'Mirror, Mirror on the wall
Who is the most accomplished of them all?'

'You are' is the tempting answer for the coach who has shared the

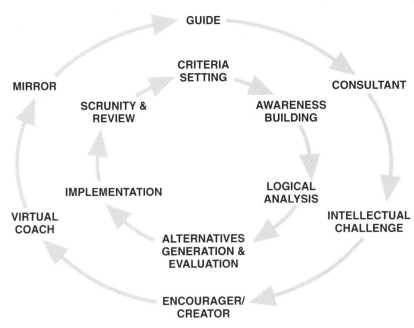

Fig. 9.1   CALAIS loop: role of the coach

struggle for mastery and the joy of success. 'I am' might be the response of the expert coach. 'What do you think?' replies the helper coach. If the coach assumes responsibility for examining and evaluating performance then she has slipped into being directive. In the *Scrutiny and Review* phase of the CALAIS loop the impetus for examination and evaluation comes from the trainee. It's her learning so it's her appraisal which matters. The coach is not absent. The coach's role is to act as a mirror. The coach reflects back what happened at the criteria setting phase and the awareness building phase, the logical analysis phase. The purpose of the mirroring is to help the trainee appreciate the progress made and to acknowledge the distance yet to go. The mirror reflects back the image without addition or adornment, only reversed so it can be seen.

There is a role for encouragement and support and warmth and concern but those feelings should not cloud the mirror. Anything else is to treat the trainee as a less than equal partner in the process, to revert to the command and control style. Having the trainee talk through what happened and what she learned, asking probing and reflective questions, listening and recapping and sharing her joy and anxiety and accomplishment. That is the challenge for the coach.

But coaching does not just occur at the one-to-one level. It also occurs with teams. Bringing teams together, helping them to develop and facilitating their interactions are all roles in which the coach is to some extent engaged.

The scout

Depending on the organisation the coach may or may not be responsible for selecting members of the team. The team may or may not have a leader. Increasingly, in project groups there is some discretion over who is a member of the team. At Hartlepool an important ingredient of success was seen to be the decision to select teams rather than ask for volunteers. At ICI Merseyside the changing composition of teams provided valuable learning. If the coach is the team leader then choosing members of the team is about seeing potential in relation to the criteria already identified. If the criteria change over time, that should prompt a reconsideration of team members. All interested parties are potential team members. Some may never become formal members of the team but that does not prevent their incorporation and inclusion.

If the coach is not the team leader but is outside the team then her task becomes one of working with the leader and the initial team members to identify any gaps or omissions and suitable replacements. If the central aim remains that of coaching, then a key criterion for selection must be that the individual wants to develop in ways which could be fostered by inclusion in the team. Having a team only some of whose members are committed to development will cause stresses in setting criteria and reviewing progress. Those who are not committed to development will be inclined to ask for, or offer, more direction than is compatible with learning. If the team exists for any significant length of time it is likely that its formal membership will change. Each change creates a new development opportunity, not just for the incomer and the team leader but all the other team members.

In addition to meeting learning needs, the composition of the team will depend on which game it is playing in Drucker's phrase (Chapter Seven). Cricket teams have different requirements from football teams or choirs or drama groups. If the organisation requires individuals with highly developed but separate proficiencies, that is different to needing flexible multi-skilled substitutes. The coach and the team need to be clear about the organisational requirements as well as their own in selecting a team.

The facilitator

The facilitator role involves managing the group dynamics at particular points in time and aiding the team to develop over time. A useful approach might be for the facilitator to utilise Tuckman's Forming, Storming, Norming, Performing, Adjourning phases as a way of mapping team behaviour over a series of short intervals. Every time the team comes together it needs to re-Form, re-Storm . . . so that it can develop and learn from its own behaviour. Within those phases, the facilitator is concerned to help the team understand its own dynamics and overcome the obstacles which prevent effective performance. In Chapter Seven the issue of problem players was recast as problem systems. Individual behaviour is a function of settings and interactions not just individual motives and attitudes.

The coach may be the facilitator or may be coaching the facilitator to the group. If the former, then in addition to facilitation, the coach is working with the team to help it facilitate itself using the CALAIS loop as an explicit map for improvement. If the latter, then the coach concentrates the CALAIS loop process on the trainee facilitator focusing on her handling of the interactions.

The pilot

Creating self-managed teams is not without risk. As we saw in the Digital example, such teams may lose their way or, if their facilitation skills are not strong enough, may be so riven by argument that they fail to make progress. In such circumstances, some organisations, including Sherwood Computer Services, have found it necessary to re-install a manager on a temporary basis. The emphasis here is on the temporary. The coach, or pilot, is only with the team for long enough to allow them to overcome their current difficulties. That time may include an intensive period of coaching as the manager equips the team to cope on their own.

The naval analogy is clear. When a pilot comes on board, she assumes responsibility for navigating the vessel through a particular set of waters. All other aspects of the ship remain under the control of the original crew. As soon as the ship is clear of those waters, the pilot returns control to the crew. Self-managed teams are at the very forefront of organisational understanding. They are so distant from command and control structures as to belong on a different planet. It is scarcely surprising that occasional difficulties result. The manager as coach needs to guard against her own willingness to define every patch of water as a 'tricky one' and assume the pilot's responsibilities too easily. Handled appropriately, taking a pilot on board is a useful learning experience. Handled badly, it has all the learning potential of seeing your keyboard commandeered by a wizard. It may produce a result, it may even result in some learning – for the wizard.

The leader and interpreter

Beyond the internal workings of the team, the manager as coach has two related responsibilities, those of interpreter and leader. In a constantly changing world, the team is regularly bombarded with new information, new insights, new ideas, new opportunities and new threats. One of the key roles of the leader is to interpret all this news. The leader needs to understand and prioritise and react appropriately. The leader as coach has to develop these skills in all members of the team. As they are at the front-line they receive the news before she does. They need to be able to appreciate what is new – and its implications – and respond accordingly. The world is changing too quickly to permit the sending of messages to HQ for evaluation and analysis. Again the technique here is an appropriate application of the CALAIS loop.

Depending on the task in hand, being a leader may mean having a dream or it may mean having a very clear set of objectives. The purpose is to ensure that the team has such a powerful sense of direction that all its members continue to move in the right direction even if they temporarily lose touch with each other or the manager. Visionaries are required when teams are being asked to tackle the unknown. Columbus was a visionary when he crossed the Atlantic. Airline pilots crossing the Atlantic today are not visionaries but their crews do appreciate knowing what is expected of them. The manager as coach needs to develop the team's skills in dreaming or objective setting. If the team is able to set its own objectives, appropriately informed by organisational objectives, then the sense of ownership and commitment will be that much stronger.

The emissary

A further organisational responsibility of the manager as coach is to manage the boundaries beyond the immediate work area. This might be seeking extra resources – either physical or financial – to enable team members to perform their responsibilities more efficiently or to tackle a new project. It may also be a question of ensuring that the

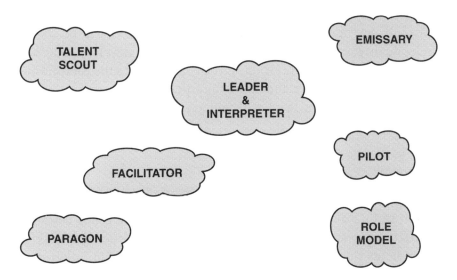

Fig. 9.2   Coaching teams: the coach's roles

manager's staff are allocated an adequate enough budget from central funds to be able to carry out the work they are expected to do. This will of course be based on the team budgets drawn up by the staff themselves. The coach will also be the person who represents the goals and achievements of the teams to higher authority. In many cases, with the trend to flattened organisation structures, that will mean putting the teams' case to the board of management. If a meeting with the board involves discussion of a particular area of expertise, the coach might take with her one or more members of staff who specialises in that area. This will give the staff members exposure to higher level management, indicate that their expertise is acknowledged and appreciated by the organisation, and provide an opportunity for the coach to develop a further range of skills in managing senior managers.

The role model

Whether or not they choose to be, coaches will be the role model for the members of their team. Hero worship is hardly appropriate in the modern flexible responsive empowered organisation. That belongs to the days of the hierarchy, but coaches are the catalyst for good behaviour and outstanding performance. The way they go about their own jobs provides an example for the team. If the coach recognises individuality, questions, listens, encourages and develops, that will become the norm for the group. If the coach mouths the rhetoric but behaves in a directive manner and reinforces differences in authority and power, then the team will understand that the changes were purely superficial.

Paragon?

It may seem that combining all the above qualities will require the coach to be a paragon or some sort of superwoman. She certainly needs to be someone who has broader vision and a wider span of skills and talents than the authoritarian manager of old. But rather than technical ability, it is the 'soft' skills that she will have to excel at. She will need to know more about handling people than how to replace a gasket. But these are the talents that wise leaders have always shown throughout history. The real art of being a coach is to recognise that the technical skills that brought the manager to this position are no longer the skills that are needed to lead and support a team. Many a would-be sales manager who thought that being a super-salesperson was the only talent needed to run a sales team has failed.

The challenge facing the coach is not an easy one. It is never a simple task to stifle the habits of a lifetime and to venture into unknown territory. Offsetting that, it can equally be argued that becoming a coach offers exciting opportunities to expand horizons and to be responsible for seeing those in your charge stretch and become more fully-rounded contributors. There can be few more rewarding jobs than that. Once they have tasted the exhilaration of such achievements, few management coaches look back with regret.

INDEX

alternatives generation in CALAIS loop 147–51, 221–2
authority and pace of change 8
autonomous work groups 71–5
awareness building in CALAIS loop 141–5, 220

Baldock, Brian 97–8
Barclays Bank 98–100, 103, 148
Barnish, Francis 64, 79
Beckett, David 211–17
Benefits Agency 21
Bennis, Warren 8, 159
Bichard, Michael 21
Black and Decker *see* Minicraft
Blanchard, Kenneth H. 132, 135–7
Boardman, Chris 162
Bowen, David 30
Brass, Jack 178–9
Briggs, Ian 43, 172, 175–7, 179
British Airways 26
British Petroleum
  four basic rules of empowerment 33–5
  Project 1990 10
British Petroleum Exploration case study 55–62
  and empowerment 68–9, 81, 136–7
Browne, John 59
Business Bodymind 161, 163, 165–6
Butler, Sir Peter 21

CALAIS loop in coaching 139–55
  and continuous improvement 152–3
  and long-term strategy 154
  and management coach 219–20, 221–3
  repetition in 152
Callanan, Gerry 93, 95
Capp, Tony 43–54
Carling, Will 96
change, pace of 1–14
  and authority 8
  and chaos 4–5
  command and control in organisations 5–6
  creative solutions for 6–7
  and empowerment 11–14
  and job security 7–8
  labour force, education of 7
  and new technology 2

chaos and pace of change 4–5
chaos theory 154–5
civil service: empowerment in 21
Clinton, President Bill 8
coach
  characteristics of 219–29
  as consultant 220
  as emissary 227
  as encourager/creator 221–2
  as facilitator 225
  as guide 219–20
  as intellectual challenger 221
  as leader and interpreter 226–7
  as mirror 222–4
  as pilot 225–6
  as role model 228
  as scout 224–5
  of teams, role of 227–8
  virtual 222
coaching
  basic loop 114
  and confidence 103–5
  and delegation 130–1, 134, 136
  in development agenda 96
  and empowerment 110–11
  feedback in 111–12
  inspiration of 96–9
  leadership model in 132–5
  and owning the system 95
  and performance of staff 94–5
  in police service 105–9
  skills, growth of 102–3
  in sport and business 93–112
  suiting the situation 113–37
  teams *see* teams
  telling style of 101–2
  and training 191–6
  see also CALAIS loop; PAPER exercise
command and pace of change 5–6
competition
  global, and pace of change 2–3
  with Japan and empowerment 16–17
Connolly, Christopher 161, 162–4, 165–71
consumer expectations, and pace of change 3
control and pace of change 5–6
Cooper, Joanna 103–4, 198, 199–202, 204–6
criteria setting in CALAIS loop 140–1, 219–20

Cumming, George 176–7

De Souza, Paul 75–7
Deighton, Trevor 78–80
Digital Equipment Ltd 15, 20
  autonomous work groups in 71–5
  job involvement in 31–3
  managers, and empowerment 69–71
  self-managed teams, problems in 75–7
Drucker, Peter 160–1, 166, 225
Dunne, Austin 24
Durcan, Jim 145, 172

Economist, The 33
employability and empowerment 24–5
employees
  coaching, and performance of 94–5
  empowerment, hidden talents in 22–4
  empowerment, opportunities in 22
  owning the system 95
  perception of managers 90–1
empowerment 11
  caution in approaching 21
  circumstances for 13–14
  in civil service 21
  and crisis 28
  definition 11–12
  and discipline 35
  distinct approaches to 30–1
  and employability 24–5
  employees' hidden talents in 22–4
  employees' opportunities in 22
  engaging in 12–13
  forms of 13
  in fresh start 25–6
  greenfield 28–30
  impact of 15–40
  and job involvement 31–3
  problems with 75–7
  and productivity 26–7
  self-managed work groups in 19–21
Evans, Judith 22–3, 94, 96, 135, 150, 193–4

feedback in coaching 142–4
feedforward in coaching 142–4

Garbutt, Ian 90–1
Golzen, Godfrey 18
Gorton, Keith 174–5
Grant, Tony 25–6
GROW model in coaching 102, 148, 215

Hackett, Dr Penny 103, 104
Handy, Charles 23
Harding, Clare 88
Hasell, Nick 41
Hemery, David 98, 103
Hersey, Paul 132, 135–7

Horton, Bob 60
Hyam, Peter 197–9, 202–6, 208

ICI 24, 103–5
  training case study 191–3, 197–209
  implementation in CALAIS loop 151–2, 222
In-Process Quality Measurement
  (IPQM) 182–3, 184, 186–8

Jackson, Bryan 28–9, 89–90
Japan, competition with 16–17
job involvement 31–3
job security and pace of change 7–8
just-in-time (JIT) manufacturing 83

Kanter, Rosabeth Moss 18

labour force education and change, pace of 7
Lawler, Edward 30
leadership and teams 167–9, 171–2
lean production 83
Lever, Chris 20, 71–4
logical analysis in CALAIS loop 146–7, 221
Lorenz, Christopher 30
Lounton, Marie-Claire 69–70

Major, PM John 8
managers
  and autonomous work groups 71–5
  as boss 89–90
  changing role of 63–91
  as coach *see* coach
  employee's perception of 90–1
  and empowerment 68–9
  expectations of 86–7
  expertise and experience of 82–3
  frustration of 83–4
  as leaders 87
  and momentum, maintaining 77–9
  operating styles, switches in 170–1
  people management 81–2
  revolution in 84–5
  as role models 88–9
  self-awareness of 169–70
Marshall, Garry 185
Maw, Simon 207
McBride, Stuart 106–9
Mills, Quinn 26
Minicraft (B & D) study 63–8, 152–3
  and manager's role 77–81
Mintzberg, Henry 83–4

Newton, Richard 33, 35
Nuclear Electric 6, 24, 28, 81, 90–1
  empowerment case study 41–54
  team building case study 173–80

organisations
  and consumer expectations 3

and global competition 2–3
and new technology 2
and pace of change 1–14
pyramid in *see* pyramids
Orrico, Ralph 27, 88–9

Page, Roy 63–8
Pantling, Shaun 20
PAPER exercise 115–30
   purpose 115–16, 118–19, 124–6
   authority 116, 120–1, 126
   practice 117, 121–2, 126–8
   evaluation 117, 122–3, 128–9
   reflection 117–18, 123–4, 129–30
Performance Consultants 98, 103, 215
Peters, Tom 10, 22
police service, new approaches in 105–9
pyramids in organisations
   flattening of 10
   horizontal 19
   inside-out 19
   inverted, at Minicraft 64–6
   inverting 18–19
   upside-down 18

Raisbeck, Ian 181–2
Rank Xerox (UK) Ltd 18, 20
   managers' roles 88–9
   productivity gains in 26–7
Ratcliffe, Ernie 207
Rothwell, Sheila 160
Royal Mail 25–6, 87
   teamwork case study 181–9

SABRE (sales-based ordering system,
      Sainsbury's) 93, 96
Sainsbury's 22–3, 150–1
   coaching studies 93–5, 135
   training case study 193–4
Savage, Adrian 115, 130–2
scrutiny and review in CALAIS loop 152,
      222–4
self-managed work groups 19–21
Sherwood Computer Services 19–20, 168
Society of Petroleum Engineers Offshore

Europe conference (1993) 2, 7
Sporting Bodymind 161, 163
Standing, Tom 55–7, 60, 68–9, 81, 136–7
Syer, John 161, 162–4

Taylor, Bernard 17
Taylor, Stephen 157
Taylorian models of organisation 17
teams 157–89
   adhocracy in 159–60
   development of 161–2
   identity in 165–7
   interaction in 164–5
   and leadership 167–9, 171–2
   managers of *see* managers
   problem players on 162–3
   sporting 160–1
   training of 191–6
   warming up and down 163–4
technology
   new, and pace of change 2
Thomas, Bob 19
Thomson, Les 58–9
Toffler, Alvin 159
Toogood, Colin 87, 183, 185–9
TOR work group (Nuclear Electric) 174
total productivity maintenance 57–9
Toyota 28–9, 89–90
training 191–6
Tuckman, 164

virtual coach 222

Walsh, Rhoda 70
W.H. Smith 21
Whitaker, David 98–9, 101–2, 110, 112
Whitmore, Sir John 98, 105
Wigston, Ian 99–100, 103
Williams, Gwyn 182–5
Williams, John 24, 201, 203, 205, 208
Woolwich Building Society: training case
      study 194–5, 210–17
Wright, Alistair 15, 22

Zelmer, Vernon 18